THE
COURAGE
TO
ACHIEVE

Why America's
Brightest Women
Struggle
to Fulfill Their Promise

●

Betty A. Walker, Ph.D.
and
Marilyn Mehr, Ph.D.

SIMON & SCHUSTER
NEW YORK ● LONDON ● TORONTO
SYDNEY ● TOKYO ● SINGAPORE

SIMON & SCHUSTER
Simon & Schuster Building
Rockefeller Center
1230 Avenue of the Americas
New York, New York 10020

10 9 8 7 6 5 4 3 2 1

Library of Congress Cataloging-in-Publication Data

Walker, Betty A.
  The courage to achieve: why America's brightest
women struggle to fulfill their promise/Betty A.
Walker and Marilyn Mehr.
    p.   cm.
  Includes bibliographical references.
    1. Hunter college. High School—Alumni—Bi-
ography.   2. Gifted girls—United States—Psychology—Case studies.   3. Success—United States—
Case studies.   4. Achievement motivation—Case
studies.   5. High school graduates—Employment—United States. I. Mehr, Marilyn. II.
Title.
LD7251.N288W35 1992
155.6'33'0973—dc20   92-20951
                                                 CIP

ISBN 0-671-73642-6

Acknowledgments

The writing of this book has been an incredible journey full of unexpected discoveries, chance meetings, endless lunches and dinners in port cities, and the deep sharing of personal stories with women of quality. We have encountered acts of kindness and generosity that were intense and heart-warming, as well as rejections and criticisms that were painful. Not once, however, have we wanted to surrender our commitment to this work. We were determined to arrive at our destination with our dream intact.

Similar to many of the women in our study, we, too, were encouraged as students to follow traditional paths. Stepping beyond familiar perimeters has been due in large measure to the encouragement of our mentors, Dr. Esther Somerfeld and Dr. Winafred Lucas, women of achievement who were resolutely convinced that each of us had talents which must be challenged and explored. They pointed the way to graduate school, advanced degrees, professorships, private practices, and finally, to little desks in isolated rooms where we began to imagine ourselves as writers. They challenged us to set out on uncharted terrain.

Once we knew that we must write about smart women's lives, there were many who doubted or sought to diminish our vision. Without devoted and passionate supporters, we might have listened to their warnings and objections and produced a far less compelling book. Our deepest gratitude to those who "got it": Collette North and Marilyn Kizziah, who offered lunch, laughter, and a wise political perspective; Lois Rice, Rose Christofileas, Joan Jensen, and Rita Blau, who gave generously of their experiences and resources; Betty and Alex Christofileas, Vivian and Al Mehr, who provided the special love and encouragement that sustained us all along the way.

The academic community has also proven a valuable resource. The University of Southern California's Faculty Research and Innovation Fund award provided seed money, and the School of Education's Educare grants allowed for the completion of the research aspect of the study. Two colleagues, Dr. Birgitte Mednick and Dr. Robert Baker, gave valuable thinking, time, and advice. Thank you for your perspective, respect for our differences, and rigorous discourse.

Approaching the Hunter High School Administration and Alumnae Association for support to conduct this research was vital to the realization of the study. From the initial conversations with Karen McCarthy, Evelyn Jones Rich, and Harriet Aufses, we encountered the kind of intellectual curiosity, open access, and encouragement that characterize the spirit of Hunter. A shower of "thank you's" to all of you, as well as to Dr. Florence Denmark and Dr. Donna Shalala at Hunter College who also gave critical endorsement to our endeavor.

The mysterious workings of the publishing world were passed on by a relay of very savvy women. Initially, when the USC News Service publicized our study, Grace Hechinger at *Glamour* magazine spotlighted our research in her education column. We were deluged by phone calls and media attention. Shortly after, Gloria Steinem recognized the value of our proposal and advised us "to write for the smartest women you know." We are grateful to both women for their recognition and seasoned advice.

Literary agent Barbara Lowenstein brought to our proposal intelligence, demanding standards, and unfailing impatience with academic abstractions. Whereas others had been supportive through agreement, Barbara challenged us through incisive and probing questions, spirited objections, honest reactions, and workable recommendations. She also introduced us to Susanne Lipsett, who balanced the intensity of New York publishing with her own West Coast style of low-key reflection, humor, and a ready understanding of how our proposal could take shape.

Through Barbara, we had the immense good fortune to meet another exceptionally smart and courageous woman, Susanne Jaffe, our editor. Her commitment to publishing this book has come from a deep reservoir of experience and knowledge. For her willingness to risk, her keen editorial judgment, her fervent and clear conception of this book, we are extraordinarily grateful.

Bringing coherence and clarity to the volume of ideas and stories we both had loaded into our steamer trunk of possibilities was an invaluable guide and friend, Josleen Wilson. Through her persistent questioning and searching intelligence she helped bring order and unity to our vast array of material. Her fascination with the lives of our subjects, her interest in the texture of their experiences, allowed us to make them as real and vibrant as we had found them in person. Our heartfelt thanks, Jos, to one of the very smart.

And finally, we extend our appreciation to the women of Hunter—those graduates and teachers, past and present—especially to those who gave so generously of their time, their thoughts, their most intimate and cherished memories. To all of you over the many decades who made this book possible, we are deeply grateful.

To our mothers and grandmothers.
Smart women all,
whose lives showed us why
this book had to be written.

CONTENTS

Introduction   13

ONE   WHAT IS SMART?   23
TWO   CRITICAL CHOICE POINTS   35
THREE   GROWING UP   53
FOUR   WITHIN THE WALLS OF HUNTER   75
FIVE   COUNSELING: THE 911 OF EDUCATION   87
SIX   CHOOSING WORK   97
SEVEN   WORKING: STRUGGLE FOR THE TOP   114
EIGHT   LOVE AND MARRIAGE   126
NINE   BALANCING ACTS   140
TEN   REENTRY   152
ELEVEN ACTIVE ENGAGEMENT   168
TWELVE CONCLUSION   179

Bibliography   183
Index   197

INTRODUCTION

In 1985 I enthusiastically applied for a grant from the University of Southern California's Faculty Research and Innovation Fund, hoping to learn why women were generally absent from the very top leadership positions in all areas, from politics to show business to academics. My associate, Dr. Marilyn Mehr, and I planned to study the lives of living graduates of Hunter College High School from the 1910s through the 1980s; Hunter High is a New York City public school whose female students were recognized according to a number of standards to be among the brightest in the nation. We reasoned that by studying Hunter women we would eliminate possible lack of intelligence or poor education as factors preventing achievement.

We felt that here at last was a way to get at what had been haunting us for a long time: why women were absent from top positions of leadership. We didn't realize, however, just how hard a task it would be or how long it would take to find answers.

As with all passionate commitments, ours had its roots in our personal lives. As a child I had been plucked out of the sixth grade of P. S. 3 in the Bronx by a principal who suggested that I take a test to attend Hunter College Junior High School, a free city school founded in 1870 for the "enrichment of girls who *might* be bright" [italics mine]. I remember my mother on the morning that I took the subway alone into Manhattan for the first time. "Now, honey," she said, buttoning my coat, "stand right next to the train door so you can push your way out when it opens. Do your best and be sure to answer all the questions right." Even though my mother knew that "answering the questions right" meant that I might leave her and the neighborhood forever, she was determined that I would have more opportunities than she had.

On that one day my future changed. I entered Hunter College Junior High and began my path via the New York City subway system to a superior education—en route to a very traditional career. I learned to survive on the El train at rush hour, determined to battle my way through the mass of humanity at 68th Street and Third Avenue and head down the block to Hunter. Frightened and awed, I scrambled up the school steps to face excellent teachers, a rigorous curriculum, and my classmates—none of whom lived in a five-flight, walk-up tenement. I knew I was a long way from home.

I dared not share my fears and insecurity about this new life with my mother, whose own education was thwarted by poverty, early marriage, and lack of encouragement. Nor did I tell my Hungarian-Gypsy grandmother, who read clusters of tea leaves to detect meaning and certainty in an unpredictable and confusing world. Yet each of them, my mother and my grandmother, had learned the bitter lessons of survival and passed them on to me daily.

I was too impressed with my special school in the smart East Side of Manhattan to listen. I turned a deaf ear to my grandmother, who admonished me, "You go to school, but you don't learn anything about real life there!" She was right, because I never got much advice about the harsh reality of living outside academic circles. I went all the way through Hunter Junior High and High School.

Then I took the traditional track and went on to Hunter College to earn a teaching certificate.

My first assignment was teaching high school English in the South Bronx. Now I was living and working about as far from my academically sheltered environment as imaginable. But during that period I learned a lot about teaching, counseling, and commitment. I was all too familiar with the consequences of poverty, inequality, and hopelessness in the lives of my family and neighbors. As a young teacher I relived it in the lives of my impoverished Puerto Rican kids who came to school without breakfast, or a night's sleep in a bed of their own.

Whenever I thought about these matters I felt helpless to change them. Then one day I met a visionary teacher who inspired me to join the fledgling United Federation of Teachers. At that point, I learned one of the most important lessons of my adult life: "If you don't like what's happening, hit the streets!" And we did! In my early twenties I became involved in the first New York City teachers' strike. I became a union shop steward in my school, sat around at local meetings and sang songs of rebellion with Al Shanker, won an award for my efforts during our successful strike and, for the first time, truly felt challenged and empowered.

Perhaps that experience awakened a dormant sense of my own possibilities. Emboldened by the teachers' strike, I was ready to take new risks. Similar to many restless people who live on the edges of continents, I moved to the other side, to California, where I received a stipend and enrolled in a summer program for training school counselors. At summer's end, the noted counselor-educator Jane Waters encouraged me to enter the graduate studies program at the University of Southern California.

I was stunned by this suggestion. In two generations, the women in my family had progressed from my grandmother,—a scared, brave peasant girl, unable to read or write,—to my mother, who left school at thirteen, married at seventeen, and used her talents to take care of less capable bosses in the garment industry,

to me, a teacher. I was part of a female heritage—rooted in brains
and barriers. Could I advance even further for a Ph.D.? Professor
Waters, without designation, served as my role model. With her
encouragement, I made a choice to change the course of my life;
I applied for the doctoral program.

Back in the mid 1960s, the USC graduate program was alive
with students who were questioning, rebelling, and challenging.
Even the check-out lines in the student bookstore were full of unruly
students arguing about the imperatives of life. It was in this program
that I first met Marilyn Mehr, a classmate who was also working
for her doctorate. We both finished the program and eventually
reached similar goals in becoming psychologists and professors at
USC. I now hold the same position in the same department at this
university that Professor Waters once did.

This process has taken time. For most of our professional years
we, as so many other women, floundered our way towards better
positions. Separately and as colleagues, we published extensively in
the professional literature. Our research and writing in these years
centered on adolescents and families in crisis. Despite these career
challenges, we still felt as individuals that we were standing in place.

We both developed private practices that increasingly focused
on bright, inquiring women intent on living fulfilling lives. While
many of our women clients came to therapy determined to make
their work more challenging and rewarding, others wanted to explore
underlying personal and emotional problems first. However, the
personal was interwoven with the vocational and educational concerns of our clients. We met them in our private offices, community
hospitals, and special programs set up in disadvantaged neighborhoods. Women of all ages and ethnic backgrounds, they worked in
banks as tellers and vice presidents; they worked in schools as secretaries and principals, and in hospitals as doctors and as medical
records clerks. They worked in law firms as attorneys and as recep-
tionists. Some had Ph.D.s, M.D.s, and J.D.s. Others had graduated
from high school and perhaps taken a vocational course. Some had
lost jobs and were out of work, while others had never been employed

outside their homes and were trying to set out on jobs. Still others were contemplating a move to a higher position or making a radical change to an altogether different line of work. All, however, were determined to better themselves personally and professionally.

We saw opportunities open up for them, and then shut off as they rose closer to the top. We sensed a growing restlessness, almost an irritation, in our friends and clients. As the nation rolled into the 1980s we were seeing more women trying to cope with the frustration and confusion they felt when promised equal opportunity and advancement, who then became stuck in midlevel jobs. Young women, in particular, felt "set up" as they left school and tried to move to the top ranks of their chosen fields.

Dr. Mehr and I had seen it in our own lives, each having gone farther than our mothers or grandmothers would have dreamed, yet each having reached some kind of stalemate.

The thought of grinding out studies for professional journals for another twenty or so years numbed me, sending me back to fantasies of returning to the union hall. Looking for action, I invited on two separate occasions Ellen Goodman, Pulitzer Prize–winning journalist from *The Boston Globe*, and Helen Caldicott, former Harvard-faculty pediatrician turned peace activist and founder of WAND (Women Against Nuclear Destruction), to speak to USC students about the issues of women and leadership. Goodman, self-contained, low-key, spoke for the first time about the "Super Woman Syndrome." She addressed the problem that women face in trying to meet everyone's expectations on their own. Caldicott, brilliant and fiery, came at it from a more global aspect and challenged women to charge forth and save the planet.

Few were interested. We seemed stranded in a spaceship halfway to the moon without a booster.

Then one Christmas Eve seven years ago everything changed. Marilyn and I, sharing a car, had left Los Angeles late, prepared to catch up with our holiday skiing party at a lodge in Mammoth Mountain. Half-way up the mountain it began snowing heavily. A trooper stopped us to warn that the upper reaches of the road were officially closed by an avalanche. He waved his hand vaguely into the snowy night, pointing us up the road to accommodations. We crept along until, magically, a tiny motel and diner appeared, a plastic Christmas tree blinking in its front window.

In the diner we ate undercooked chicken and overdone mashed potatoes, watching snow and sleet pelt the window. To while away the time, we told each other childhood tales from other holidays. After dinner, we drifted into the small lobby and settled into a couple of chairs in front of a fire. The other snow-bound travelers had retired to their rooms, so we felt quite alone and isolated. Our casual reminiscences grew more reflective, as late-night conversations often do. Halted in midjourney, we were also suspended for a night in midlife.

We began to talk about our families and to remember female figures in our lives who had paved the way for us. I told Marilyn about my immigrant grandmother, Rosie Hagen, the tea-leaf reader who had left her nameless Hungarian village by herself at the age of thirteen for an unknown country, and after arriving in America worked most of her life making artificial flowers and rolling Havana Supremes in a cigar factory. After her second husband died Rosie fed her children by working an extra job in the school cafeteria, where she was permitted to take home leftovers. My grandmother had never gone to school, but her daughter, Bertha Anna, made it through the eighth grade.

"My mother was a very intelligent child," I recalled. "By the time she was twelve she had mastered shorthand and typing. That's when her stepfather, Rosie's short-lived second husband, insisted she leave school to get a job in the garment district. Mom was as smart as I ever was, but nobody stood up for her."

Bertha Anna did what she had to. Through her secretarial skills she worked her way up in McCreery's department store. She was a teenage mother during the Depression, then divorced. She worked hard to take care of me, her only child.

"Did your grandmother always live with you?" Marilyn asked.

"I always remember her living with us. Mom went out to work, Grandma spent the afternoons in the kitchen reading fortunes for all the neighborhood grandmothers, and I studied Latin and geometry at my desk in the corner." My grandmother came back to me like a ghost.

Marilyn recalled her own Mormon grandmother to life and heard again the many messages she sent almost subliminally over the years. "I can see my grandmother in the kitchen," she said, "starched white apron strapped around her waist, moving from counter to stove to table, like a dancer, constantly in motion. She seemed to step to an invisible beat. I always thought she had her own rhythm, that she learned it as a child growing up on the western plains."

Marilyn was the first female in her family to finish college. She faced some painful choices in creating a life for herself. In her first year at college she wanted to be a writer but, worried about the insecurity of the artist's life, she took her counselor's advice and chose education instead. She became a schoolteacher, but felt she wasn't cooking on all burners. She began to work her way through the USC doctoral program to become a psychologist. At that point, however, she was forced to go head-to-head with the Mormon teachings that her family lived by. Wrenching herself away from the accepted "program" meant causing pain to her parents and accepting their criticism and disappointment. She confronted her family and herself, and ultimately followed her own beliefs.

In both of our families, each successive generation of women had managed to go far beyond the previous one. Our foremothers had done well by us, and we understood it was our job to do well for them. Marilyn and I realized how deeply our connections to other women ran through our lives, like a huge underground network of tunnels carrying memories and messages.

In the course of the long night, we talked at length about the times that our female ancestors had made—or been forced to make—critical decisions that changed the course of their lives. The decision to leave school, work at arduous low-paying jobs, have a baby, get married or get divorced—each point seemed to have a massive effect on the outcome of their lives.

This was the first time I had recognized the strange coincidence of the women in my family coming of age. "Think of that," I said to Marilyn, "a life-forming decision came for my grandmother, my mother, and then myself at the same age of thirteen." Rosie came to America, Bertha Anna quit school and went to work, and I leapt from the South Bronx into the glittering world of Manhattan. This insight was one of many that came to each of us over the course of the weekend.

Finally, we called it quits, exhausted by our travels and explorations, but full of the stories of mothers and grandmothers. In the morning, the rumor circulated among the breakfast tables that the avalanche would be cleared by noon. We lingered over coffee.

"You know, I've been thinking," Marilyn began. "What happened to all those Hunter girls, your junior and senior high school classmates, all of those superstars? Do you know?"

I didn't have a clue. And if we were all supposedly so smart as to have been chosen for that special education, I should have heard of at least some of them as they progressed upward toward the top of their fields. These women should have been running the world. What had happened to them, some of the best and the brightest New York City had to offer?

The penny dropped. Marilyn's question about my classmates precisely dovetailed with the irritating discomfort of these past months—why were women invisible at the top? If we could study the life course of one well-defined group of women, we might be able to answer the mystery for most, if not all, women.

A woman doesn't need an IQ test to know she is smart. We have met and worked with women from every social, ethnic, and economic background. Some women know they are smart because they have been tested; others just look around them and know they are faster, sharper, and more keen than many people.

But we felt if we could discover why bright women with quality educations are unable to blaze new trails to the top, then we could generalize from the findings to help provide a template for all women.

After my ski trip, I ransacked my office at USC, looking for a folder of research grant applications. My office decor is the subject of some amusement to my students and colleagues. It is cluttered with my souvenirs, a Charlie Chaplin poster I bought years ago in Paris, a kaleidoscope to gaze through whenever I feel moody or frustrated by some Neanderthal colleague. My filing cabinet is decorated with stickers proclaiming "peace," "justice," and "free choice." I realize that I'm an idealist living in an age of technology, but I persist. To the front door of my office are pinned weekly cartoons, attesting that life is a serious occupation but intrinsically absurd. These irreverent handbills are my attempts to provoke some response from my more conservative students.

Surrounded by my mementos, I could almost hear the voices of my Hunter classmates. Their discussions, full of ardor and conviction, rose up and cascaded over me. I was energized by these memories and ready to throw myself full-throttle into the research fray. "Discontent" was my middle name. It was a familiar, good feeling, and I ventured forth into the research marketplace with the cheers of my old friends on the picket line, my revolutionary classmates of the 6os and my former Hunter classmates ringing in my ears.

ONE

WHAT IS SMART?

Am I really the smartest?
— SHARON, *class of '73*

In a modern climate of equal access and opportunity, women would expect to settle in beside their male counterparts at the top. This has not happened in any noticeable way, and little has been done to find out why. In our survey, highly intelligent and well-qualified women were asked, for the first time, to tell us how they had put their talents and resources to work and why more of them were not leaders.

Only a few studies have scientifically compared female achievement to male achievement. The benchmark is a now-famous investigation by Lewis Terman, professor of psychology at Stanford University, in 1925. Terman tracked the achievements of intellectually gifted men and women from childhood through adulthood. He found that from the first grade through college, women equaled or excelled men in school. The girls did slightly better in language usage, and the boys above age nine did slightly better in math, but, overall, *there was no significant difference* in their academic achievements.

In later life, however, while the boys went on to achievements consistent with their abilities, the girls failed to live up to the researcher's predictions for their development. Only 48 percent of the gifted women were employed, and one-third of these held clerical jobs. The girls who had been slightly superior to boys in language usage, especially those deemed the most talented writers, as adults did not rise to the surface of the literary world. Nearly all of the participants who went on to become eminent writers were men.

Over the next half century, Terman's findings stood unexplored and unchanged. Researchers continued to report the wide discrepancies in adult achievement between men and women. In 1979, researcher C. M. Callahan showed that while girls earned higher grades in school, men wrote more books, earned more degrees, produced more works of art, and made more contributions in all professional fields. In 1987, Professor Sally M. Reis from the University of Connecticut summed up the conclusions of many researchers: "In almost all professional fields and occupations, men have overwhelmingly surpassed women in both the professional accomplishments they achieve and the financial benefits they reap."

The question clearly was not if but *how* and *when* does the cycle of lower female achievement begin? Some researchers tried to use Terman's work to prove that women lacked mathematical ability, but in fact no research has ever found any inherent reason for women to lag behind in any subject.

Back in 1925, Terman believed that the missing excellence factor in adult women was due to lack of motivation and opportunity, rather than any lack of ability. Over the years, others have tried to discover why adult women might lose their motivation, citing variously and excessive need for approval, learned dependency, and narrow definitions of femininity that require a woman to avoid competitiveness and power. In order to achieve, they said, a woman must almost become a mutation of her female role—she must live a man's life in a woman's body.

Academically speaking, this was where things stood when my coauthor, Dr. Marilyn Mehr, and I began our Hunter study. It would land us in the center of a national controversy and ultimately help shape a new concept of the female life cycle.

We selected Hunter High School as our study laboratory because it is an urban public school whose student population better reflected society as a whole than might students from a select private school. Even though in the early years of the school most students were white girls from average-income families, Hunter has since widened its base to a multicultural student body and, since 1974, has also included boys.

The basic ground rules for entry to Hunter Junior and High School today are these: sixth-graders must score at least 74 percent in a standardized reading test, and at least 94 percent in standardized mathematics. They must be recommended by their school principal and must then pass a special Hunter exam in English and math.

WHAT IS SMART?

IQ tests are no longer used to qualify Hunter applicants, but in the past applicants were required to have an IQ of 130 or above. The average IQ of Hunter students today probably hovers around 140. An IQ rating above 130 places an individual in the intellectually superior range. "Intellectually superior" is defined as the top 2 percent of individuals taking the standardized IQ test. By mathematical percentages individuals are clustered according to IQ on a bell-shaped curve: very low (2 percent), below average (16 percent), average (64 percent), above average (16 percent), and superior/gifted (2 percent).

Over much of this century intelligence has been seen as a single trait that might be measured—like standing on a scale to see how much you weigh. In 1906 the French psychologist Alfred Binet created the first widely used "scale" to measure intelligence. Binet himself viewed intelligence as a variety of mental abilities, such as abstract reasoning, verbal skills, and spatial judgment. Later, an English psychologist, Charles Spearman, added the idea that there was an underlying "general intelligence" to all these abilities. In 1912, a German psychologist, William Stern, coined the term "intelligence quotient" (IQ). In 1916, Lewis Terman produced an IQ test based on Binet's original scale. Terman called it the "Stanford-

Binet," and this is the test that became widely used for intelligence testing throughout the United States. An individual's IQ is determined by dividing "mental age," as determined by the test score, by chronological age, and multiplying the result by 100 to avoid any fraction. Thus, intelligence, narrowly conceived, can be measured by tests that give a numerical intelligent quotient (IQ).

Today, most educators and scientists believe that standard IQ tests measure only a fraction of human intelligence and that IQ may have small impact on how successful a person is in life. The trend nowadays is to look at intelligence in broader terms. John Horn, a psychologist at the University of Southern California, says, "What we see as intelligence, and tend to regard as a whole, is in fact a mosaic of many different units." In this view, intelligence is measured by how well individuals succeed in putting their strengths into play in the society around them.

The U.S. Office of Education acknowledges that children capable of high performance may show general intellectual ability; aptitude in a specific subject; leadership qualities; talent in the arts; the ability to think creatively; or exceptional physical capabilities. These talents may be displayed singly or in combination.

Another theorist and psychologist, Harvard's Howard Gardner, supports the idea of a broad range of traits: "I believe that as long as we have a narrow definition of intelligence—a very scholastic definition—most kids are going to think they're stupid, and they're going to miss the fact that they may have a lot of abilities that could be important vocationally and avocationally. Enlarging the concept of intelligence, and realizing that people may not have the school intelligence but may have other equally important ones—I think that would be an enormously valuable thing to happen . . . to think that there is a last word is what's wrong with most intelligence theorists."

Gardner has been criticized for equating talent with intelligence and for seeing everything good in human behavior as intelligence. Academic purists argue that his ideas can backfire. Chester Finn, chairman of a federal testing program, says, "It's all right if kids don't get the right answer as long as they're creative in their approach. But is that good? I firmly believe that every young American ought to have some idea who Thomas Jefferson and Abraham Lincoln are, and I don't care whether their greatest strength is playing the ukelele or skating backwards on the ice."

Controversies about the nature of intelligence revolve around the age-old dilemma of environment versus genetics: does intelligence come with the gene packet—you've either got it or you don't—or is it an acquired competence sensitive to environmental abuse or encouragement? As always, there are good arguments for both.

Even as educators and psychologists war over the roots of intelligence, they agree that there's more to being smart than taking a test and getting a high IQ score.

It seems solidly noncontroversial to say that simple problems that are approached and solved in the same way by everyone—such as locating the nearest neighborhood school—probably require little of what we call intelligence.

Evaluating the quality of that school requires greater intelligence. Power, speed of response, memory, transferring learning to an unfamiliar situation, basic common sense, insight and wisdom, motivation, and creativity all relate to intelligence.

Good grades in that school do not guarantee either social competence or practical intelligence, what we call "common sense." Many women who do not believe they are "gifted" will admit that maybe they are "smart" or have "common sense," as if these were lesser traits. In fact, although these may seem to exist separately, it's entirely possible to be both highly intelligent and also have common sense.

Other current trends incorporate culture and social skills as a part of intelligence. Social intelligence concerns a person's ability to solve problems that arise in the world around her. In other words, how an individual adapts to or shapes the environment, or forges a totally new setting, indicates intelligence.

As long ago as Aristotle, philosophers have recognized that intelligence includes something beyond the ability to learn and absorb knowledge. This something else resides in the human will and emotion: the desire to achieve, the confidence and belief in one's own abilities. Confidence clearly can be altered through life experience. For some people confidence appears in babyhood and seems able to stand up to any corrosive life experience. When desire and will and emotion enter the picture, any theory of intelligence becomes more reflective of the complexities of human capabilities.

Being smart, then, means many things. It's that special something which many women possess. Perhaps it never showed on their report cards, but it is visible in their daily lives. It manifests itself in their approach to others and their ability to solve problems in life.

Some women know they are smart because they have been tested and told they have high IQs. Others have never been measured or informed, yet know it anyway. There are those who believe they've got brains, but not brilliance. Some who say that they're no genius but acknowledge their sharpness and acuity. Some say they lack savvy in making certain important choices, but know they're intelligent.

Other people may be aware of a woman's intelligence and comment on how quick or clever she is. I am reminded of an older woman I know opening up a new VCR with a complicated computerized handset, definitely not user-friendly. She glanced at the handbook, which seemed to be written in Japanese, hooked up all the wires, and immediately punched up the program she wanted to record. The equipment was off and running. To this day, no one else in her household has been able to master the VCR. Her family says she has been doing things like that all her life, although she has no idea what kind of IQ she has, nor did she have an extensive education. "She's very impatient," her sister told me. "She can't stand to slog through directions and things. She just barges in and does it."

Whether or not a woman has completed high school or college, whether she is book-smart, street-smart, common-sense smart, a smart woman feels a uniqueness, a something special about herself. She feels she may have a lot more to offer than is generally recognized. To sum up, every female who has ever swallowed hard and pretended to know less knows what it means to be smart—for a girl.

A WOMAN'S LIFE

When it comes to research on the subject, the life cycle of adult women is almost a blank canvas. Earlier studies that established a timetable for adult development were mainly done by men studying other men. Pioneering work of theorists such as Daniel Levinson, Gail Sheehy, George Vaillant, and Erik Erikson showed us that just as children go through specific stages of development, the adult personality also continues to develop according to fairly predictable internal rhythms.

These researchers divided the adult life span into stages, marked by specific crossroads or "crises." (A crisis in this sense is not a catastrophe, but a crucial period of vulnerability an heightened potential as a person moves from one stage to the next. The person who gets stuck in a stage and fails to move on might possibly develop some degree of emotional or physical illness or, at the very least, remain stunted and frustrated, unable to grow further.)

Levinson calculated that each period would last no longer than seven or eight years. Erikson, by contrast, said there were three stages of adulthood, and Sheehy roughly divided the adult life cycle into five decades. But most theorists would agree that adolescence, young adulthood, adulthood (maturity), middle age, and old age constitute common periods of adult development.

From the beginning, Levinson surmised that a woman's psychological development might be different from a man's, but he did not pursue this line of investigation by including women in his work. Sheehy had interviewed both men and women and concluded that the two sexes march to a different drummer in terms of *timing*, but their fundamental steps of development were the same. Others have also believed that women progress through the life cycle in ways different from men.

Yet the unique passage of adult women through the stages of the life cycle remained largely unexplored and uncharted. We thought that if we could unravel the critical junctures of bright women's lives, we might see what had happened along the way to hold them back from positions of power and leadership. We want to see if certain phases in smart women's lives were consistent enough to evoke a pattern that might be applicable to women generally.

DAUGHTERS OF THEIR TIME

A basic tenet of life-cycle theory is that emotional tasks tick off according to an internal rhythm, regardless of what happens in the outside world. However, theorists admit that every stage also incorporates external aspects. A major external event—a war, depression, loss of a parent, or other trauma—can block or slow down the stage. The culture itself has a tremendous influence on women's development.

No one knows for certain how these internal and external factors act together. Like George Elder, who studied and wrote *Children of the Great Depression,* we believe that the interaction between an individual and the Zeitgeist, or cultural spirit, of the particular society in which she or he grows up has a powerful effect on the outcome of her or his life. Perhaps external factors play an even larger role than previously recognized, particularly on the lives of women.

The Hunter graduates gave us a unique opportunity to look at external aspects because we could include women from different decades and observe their lives *against the society in which they came of age.* This historical perspective added a powerful dimension to the study. We knew that external social factors had changed dramatically over the twentieth century—would a woman's life cycle be affected accordingly?

We wondered, too, if the stages of a woman's life might also be influenced by the spirit of earlier decades, when her female ancestors came of age, just as our own lives were so deeply connected to the experience of our mothers and grandmothers. We considered how messages could be telegraphed over generational wires through stories, admonitions and examples.

THE HUNTER STUDY

Figuring out how to cover so much territory in one study was difficult. I called the study "An Innovative Developmental Theory Specific to Women." We had two main goals: first, to describe the lives of a group of identified bright women to discover what stages they went through in adult life. Second, to learn if the era in which they grew up, their families, and the education they received altered their cycle of development.

When I approached the Hunter administration, I was surprised to learn that I was the first to try to find out if quality education for smart girls had made a significant difference in the way they led their lives. In New York, I met with Dr. Karen McCarthy; who at the time was the highly supportive and enthusiastic director of the Hunter College Campus Schools, of which Hunter High was a part. I also contacted Dr. Florence Denmark, noted professor and researcher at Hunter College, former president of the American Psychological Association and former president of Psychology of Women, a division of the APA. Both gave generously of their time and thinking, and opened doors. In addition, I met with Donna Shalala, then president of Hunter College and Campus schools, who offered her own favorable nod to the study. With these endorsements, the Hunter High School Alumnae Association agreed to turn over their mailing lists to us, and we were also given access to the high school archives.

We designed a questionnaire that included 130 questions in four categories: simple demographics (What do you do for a living, married, kids? etc.); questions that would divulge personality, attitudes, and beliefs; and questions about educational and life experiences. The questionnaire ended with a section where participants were asked to describe their most vivid memories of their Hunter experience in a brief essay.

Altogether, we mailed over 1,250 questionnaires and received almost 600 fully developed replies, representing graduates from 1910 through the 1980s. Then we began the analysis.

"GIFTED WOMEN FAIL TO MEET POTENTIAL"

The results shocked us. While a few Hunter graduates had gathered honors and achievements at the top of their fields, overall, most had fared no better in their careers than female high school and college graduates from nongifted programs. Ninety-two percent of the Hunter women had completed college, but few held advanced degrees.

Most worked, or combined work and homemaking (73 percent). From the 1920s through the 1950s, two-thirds of them worked outside the home. Beginning in the 1960s, the number increased to 85 percent; in the 1970s, to 95 percent. Yes, women worked, but remained stagnated at middle or lower levels of employment. Almost half (46 percent) had become teachers and educators; another quarter (28 percent) were social workers,—both fields consistent with sexual stereotypes. Relatively few had entered the fields of medicine (5 percent) or engineering (5 percent).

What had been the purpose of this incredibly enriched educational program provided to highly intelligent girls? It was as though NASA had trained its astronauts for a space flight, then given them jobs as PBX operators transferring telephone calls.

TANTALIZING CLUE

In hundreds of essays, one comment stood out in startling clarity, as if the women had all rehearsed and written their replies together. Almost unanimously, whether they were ninety-two or twenty-two, the women denied that they had superior intelligence. "I am not really that smart, I am average," was a running theme. Despite the fact that they had been tested and told they ranked in the *top 2 percent of the population*, they were almost universally uncomfortable with the idea they they were smart.

Some were embarrassed, and some annoyed, by the term "gifted," which had been added to the Hunter mandate in the 1950s. One said: "I regard the labeling 'gifted' as presumptuous." Some said they felt uncomfortable with the word because it implied they were better than other women. Helene, class of '62, said, "I came from a working-class family. To me, Hunter was elitist. I always thought this message that we were intellectually gifted was disgusting. It was intellectual snobbery."

A few acknowledged their abilities, but said that superior intelligence had kept them from fitting in with family and friends outside of Hunter, so they viewed it as more of a burden than an asset. They felt "different" from other people. Rosemarie, class of '69, said, "I knew I was pretty smart, but I thought of it in the typical excluded 'smart kid' syndrome of having other people be mean to me because of it."

Once Rosemarie arrived at Hunter, she still carried the fear that someone would tease her for being bright. "I knew I had the top score on the admissions test, but I kept it a secret. I wasn't going to take a chance on being the weird one again, no thank you. I kept a low profile."

Hunter itself seemed to foster feelings of inadequacy in some students. Even Cynthia, one of the top Hunter grads of the class of '67, remembered moments of self-doubt. "My family had always told me I was bright. I always knew I was smart because even in a class full of gifted students, I was at the top of it. My mother had my IQ tested when I was a preschooler, but I didn't know the score, because they didn't tell at that time. I remember in a moment of great despair I went to our class adviser, a wonderful Latin teacher, and said, 'Oh, please tell me my IQ. I feel so terrible.' He said, 'Well, I would say if all the people in the world are your body, you are somewhere around your neck.' At first, I was relieved, then wondered why I wasn't at the top of my head."

Sharon, class of '73, said, "At Hunter, nobody was going to tell you what a smart thing you were. Everybody was very smart. But there was always this lingering 'Am I really the smartest?' I have a friend who grew up in the South. She was always the smartest one where she was. The cutest and smartest. Her sense of self is much stronger than mine."

Roxanne, class of '43, always tried her best, but still carried a lingering fear of not being good enough. "No one ever guessed how insecure I felt because I was top of the class. Friends envied and admired me. School helped bring out my potential but I walked in trepidation."

Even though the Hunter women did not suffer from any noticeable lack of self-esteem, only a few were able to admit that they knew they were bright and were proud of it. Growing up, they had received mixed messages about their intelligence, ranging from "social elitism" to "feeling different" to being teased and abused by their families and peers for their brains. Some felt the added pressure of never feeling quite smart enough. Overall, it appeared that the Hunter women lacked a positive and realistic assessment of their own strengths and talents.

This finding gave us an unexpected clue to what might lie underneath the missing excellence factor. Excellence requires that people recognize and "own" their specialness; that they view intelligence as a clearly positive trait. Without such recognition, women can never imagine how their talents might be used in a larger theater. If smart women do not acknowledge their abilities, they will never set high goals. Historian Joseph Campbell often speaks of the hero's journey, and we know that he is speaking of men. With few notable exceptions, women seldom see themselves as "heroes" in adventures of their own making. If they cannot envision themselves as leading players, they will be satisfied with supporting roles. Too many of the Hunter women did not have, or were not willing to acknowledge, a vision of themselves as special.

After analyzing the questionnaires it was time for the second part of the study to kick in: we wanted to interview the women in person. It was in their stories, told in their own words, that we hoped that some of the mysteries of the female life cycle would be revealed, along with answers to the missing excellence factor.

• TWO •

CRITICAL
CHOICE POINTS

I did whatever had to be done.
—ROXANNE, class of '43

After nearly a year of research, surveys, and questionnaires, Dr. Mehr and I flew to New York to meet some of the Hunter women face to face. Altogether, in addition to the more than 1250 questionnaires sent out, we also conducted forty lengthy, in-depth, taped or filmed interviews carried out at the college or in the homes of some of the older graduates, graduates from every decade of this century. From these, we would eventually select a representative sampling to speak for all of the women in our study.

When we began, we did not expect to find any perfectly consistent pattern to their lives. Yet from beneath the complex layering of details in each woman's life certain common themes emerged.

As a whole, the Hunter women we interviewed were a picture of robust emotional health. They saw themselves as idealistic, sensitive towards others, ambitious, and independent. They were realistic, yet tended to be perfectionists. They were neither lonely nor loners. Most described themselves as self-starting and energetic, but not particularly aggressive. Overall, their outlook on life was generally positive and upbeat.

Throughout childhood and adolescence they had matched boys grade for grade, but in adult life, like other women across the country, they had stopped short of the top. In fact, most of them had never gotten near the top.

Many were aware that they had not used their abilities to the fullest, but most were philosophical about the compromises they had made. Phyllis, a 1958 grad, was typical: "I always thought I would have a marvelous career in the theater, following in the footsteps of Helen Hayes and Uta Hagen. But I was scared to death that I wouldn't be able to earn a living as an actress or a writer, and that the world of the theater was too unreal to sustain me. I've found other ways to express myself, though, by teaching children and writing for them."

How does an adult woman choose one path over another? Learn to value one aspect of life and discard another? The answer did not readily surface, because most of the Hunter women were oblivious to the undercurrents that had shaped their lives. They spoke of vague feelings of "not fulfilling their potential," but in the same breath said that in the main they led satisfying, full lives.

THE SPIRIT OF THEIR TIMES

We asked everyone to recall the eras in which they grew up. We wanted to learn how Zeitgeist, or the social spirit of their times, shaped their goals and affected the choices they made.

Regina, a 1914 graduate, stated the case for the older graduates when she said that in her day "the lines of propriety were tightly drawn. We were expected to be good wives and mothers—women our families could be proud of. The social framework of my youth certainly tried to dictate our behavior."

Every woman we interviewed who had come of age in the 1930s cited the Great Depression as the significant event in her life. In times of economic distress, families tended to put their money toward a son's education, at the expense of their daughter's schooling. Several Hunter women who were ready for college during the Depression told us that their fathers couldn't, or wouldn't, help pay for their schooling. One woman, who had looked forward to her college freshman year in 1933, said, "I remember my father telling me that if I 'really had it' I would find a way to pay for school myself. Perhaps he's right. I guess I just didn't have enough of what it takes. Instead, I took a quickie course at business school so I could get one of the better office jobs."

Many of the Hunter women of the 1930s had to take menial jobs just to finish high school. Others had to quit. Later, in college, many changed their majors after the first or second year, from subjects they loved to subjects that would help them get one of the few jobs available to women of that period. Kitty, class of '33, said, "My deep love of English had to be renounced in favor of a math major so I could learn accounting and get a job as a bookkeeper."

World War II was the second monumental event that Hunter women recognized as significant. The Depression and the war had almost equal weight in terms of importance, but weighed in on opposite ends of the scale. The Depression instilled fear and withdrawal; the war generated excitement and opened up new possibilities for women.

"Brains and gender didn't matter one way or the other during the Second World War," one 1944 graduate said. "It was easy to get work and we were expected to. Under the banner of 'God and country' I joined the war effort and went to work in an airplane factory. When the war ended, I was dismissed from my job, along with the women I worked with."

In 1945, women were pressured to return home in order to open up job opportunities for men. The media now began to idealize the homemaker-mother but, although many women left their jobs and returned to the hearth, it wasn't as easy to stuff the genie back into the bottle. They still carried a vision of the importance of work with them. It may be more than coincidence that their daughters would emerge in the 1960s full of the resentment and outrage that their mothers may have suppressed.

Christine, a 1957 graduate, had been six years old and attending elementary school in Brooklyn when the war ended. "My mother was unique among my classmates. In many ways, she was a fabulous role model. She always worked to support me, but she hadn't finished high school. She waited tables all her life. By her example I always knew I could take care of myself. On the other hand, because of her own limited experience in the world, my mother's maximum dream was that I finish college and become an elementary school teacher, which was what Hunter gave me the opportunity to do."

In the 1950s the society seemed to close down again. The decade was repressive in various ways. A Hunter woman who graduated from college in 1952 described it this way: "Just about all my friends who had college degrees worked, if they worked at all, in the customary fields of teaching, library, or social work. If you didn't have a college education you could work in a restaurant or in an office, depending on your clerical skills. That was about it. If you didn't need the income, you could stay home and be a housewife, which is what I did."

Ingrid, who graduated in 1953, enrolled in college, but dropped out in her senior year to get married. "I started having babies right away. For reasons I don't quite understand the goal was always marriage, family, housekeeping. Eventually my brain turned to broccoli, and I went back and became a schoolteacher. I feel I've had a rich and fulfilling life, and yet I've never been a risk-taker. I don't know why."

Helene, who turned fifteen in 1960, remembered how that decade seemed to her: "That fall semester when I was fifteen I became involved in the Kennedy campaign. That was a real turning point for me. My mother thought I was nuts. I went down to Kennedy headquarters by myself and signed up. I would go every day after school. Then when I got involved in antiwar activities and civil-rights demonstrations it was very divisive in my family. Oh, my goodness. My mother would talk on the phone to her mahjongg cronies about how her daughter was a Communist. I went to

Washington one weekend; she lied to her friends about where I was. She was so ashamed. It ruptured family realtionships.

"For me, *The Feminine Mystique* was an eye-opening, wonderful book. It all resonated, I think, because I had gone to Hunter. They drummed it into your head all the time that being a woman had nothing to do with your brains. Friedan was saying the same thing, but society hadn't caught up. I found it hard to know what to do with myself. The world hadn't changed enough."

The 1970s brought high technology and the entrenchment of the nuclear age. But the 1960s legacies had made an indelible impact on the lives of women. Joyce, who graduated from Hunter High School in 1982, expressed confusion over what lies ahead. "I know I'm supposed to do something with my life, that other women have opened up the roads for me. I'm career-oriented, but I'm not sure exactly what I want to do. Talking about being black and coming from Harlem sounds like so much rationale, excuses nobody wants to hear. I don't want to give the impression that I'm some poor victim blaming everybody and everything in the world around me. But I wonder if I can truly get where I want and what it will cost me."

Toni, who came of age in the high-rolling 1980s, adds another element to the confusion: "Both of my parents are very successful. My dad wants me to succeed at something, but he doesn't really give me any direction. It's like, sure, go do it, but nobody tells me how. I feel like I'm going to explode. How am I supposed to outdo my parents? My social life and my material possessions are really important to me. My mother tells me that if I want the standard of living I've grown up with I'll have to marry a rich man. I'd like to earn it for myself, but I'm afraid I won't be able to."

THE BIG SWITCH

Overall, we saw a fairly steady rise in women's achievements, decade by decade, from 1910 through the 1980s, which was consistent with the social changes that have permitted women more access to better jobs. We saw something else, too.

At the beginning of the century only 5 percent of the Hunter women said that society's expectations or limitations posed a problem for them—even though society stringently restricted their roles. Less than 10 percent said that expectations of their parents were a problem—even though their parents expected them *not* to have a career. Nor did they have a problem living up to their own expectations. These graduates described themselves as less assertive and less ambitious, but happier and more tolerant of their circumstances than women of the later decades. They were more likely to acknowledge that they were smart, and when asked if they had experienced social rejection because of the label, everyone said "no." In responding to the question "Was being brighter than most people a problem for you?" they also said "no."

By 1980, 58 percent said that society's expectations were a problem, and 34 percent said the expectations of their parents troubled them. Even more significant, 74 percent in the 1980s now said they had a problem living up to their own expectations.

We believe these rising statistics reflect to some extent the willingness of younger women to acknowledge their abilities and speak about their real feelings. But there was more than a raising of consciousness at work here.

At the beginning of the century, women were not expected to compete for and assume positions of power and leadership. Neither the society at large nor the women themselves expected it. Over the last three decades, however, opportunities and expectations for women have increased significantly. Yet graduates today describe themselves as considerably less happy than women from the earlier decades.

Why, with more opportunity, do younger women appear less happy and less satisfied? The answer may lie in the tendency many women have to blame themselves if they are unable to reach the top in what is perceived as a climate of opportunity. One of the startling differences we see between women and men that follows them unerringly from childhood into adult life is the way they explain failure. Almost universally, when a man fails, he looks at the people and the circumstances around him and attaches blame on these external sources; when a woman fails she looks no further than herself. Many of the Hunter women blamed themselves for every "misstep," for every opportunity or decision that didn't work out. If they failed—to finish college in the Depression, to advance in their careers, to nurture their husbands and children—they consistently said if they had tried harder, been more ambitious, sacrificed more, they would have succeeded. Seldom did they blame their parents, the society, their spouses, or their teachers for any lack of success.

Social change offered increased hope and greater opportunity; yet whenever the promises of society were not kept and the new dreams went unrealized, the younger Hunter women felt turmoil and despair. They appeared to expect to succeed and to succeed quickly, and were often unprepared for the obstacles they encountered, and were often frustrated by them.

Today, while most Hunter women admit that they have more control over their lives and careers, others commented that they really didn't think things had changed much, that social pressures still governed the lives of women. A graduate from the class of 1929, looking back over most of the century, said that in her view women's roles had changed for the worse. "Women today are expected to do everything, but nobody tells them how."

UNFULFILLED POTENTIAL

Most of the Hunter women had made productive successful lives for themselves. Their self-esteem was intact and healthy. Yet a dominant theme throughout the study—across all decades and regardless of their opinion about their smartness or level of achievement—was the sense that they had not lived up to their "possibilities."

Many have argued that talented men do not necessarily reach their potential either. The salient point is that men, smart or not, occupy the very top positions of power and influence throughout the world.

One of the older graduates, seventy-one-year-old Millie, said that by the standards set for her generation she was "considered a success." "I was a Phi Beta Kappa graduate of Hunter College, and taught at the college level for six years. After I got married, we moved to the suburbs and raised a family. I was well known and admired for community work. When my husband died in 1966 I was fifty years old. I began teaching at the Bronx High School of Science, and remained there until I retired. It looks like I have a good track record of achievement, yet I feel unfulfilled and dependent, incapable of fulfilling the dreams of my youth."

Her feelings echo down the decades. A 1968 graduate could have been her twin: "I wish I'd had more help setting career goals as a teenager. This feeling persists. I don't feel I've adequately trained or used my potential yet to the fullest."

Many Hunter women said that they wanted to do something, but didn't know what. Sometimes they knew what, but didn't know *how*. Inside them were gifts they had never used. Women who feel this sense of unexpressed potential may also feel lonely and isolated. Their feelings mirrored those of women we saw in our private practices and classrooms who also felt they were not using their brains and talents to the fullest.

CRITICAL CHOICE POINTS

As we listened to and reviewed each interview, it became clear that women do not advance through the life cycle as if it were a set of stairs, each stage marked by a landing. The stages of a woman's life were more like a braid, the previous strand woven into the next one, making the periods of growth difficult to detect. All life experiences were woven into the plait to form a pattern of development.

To further complicate the passage, women seemed to move back and forth in the life stages. As they did so, they confronted pivotal moments when they had an opportunity to make a choice that shaped their futures. As the Hunter women looked back, these moments lit up as if someone had shone a spotlight on them. They were so important to the outcome of each woman's life that we began to call them "critical choice points." Whether to marry, to divorce, to become pregnant, to continue school, work, change jobs—each choice caried monumental consequences. There could be several of these in any given stage of a woman's life.

For example, if we accept that there are fives stages of an adult woman's life cycle—adolescence, young adulthood, adulthood, middle age, old age—then within each stage several choice points may occur.

An adolescent must make decisions about sexuality, leaving home, quitting school, going on to school, and so on. Uncanny similarities concerning critical choice points around age twelve and thirteen were seen across the spectrum of our study. Toni's parents divorced when she was twelve and she had to choose between her parents. When Joyce, class of '82, graduated from Hunter Elementary School at age twelve she was told she would have to retake the Hunter exam before she would be allowed to enter the junior high school (usually an automatic promotion). Joyce felt discriminated against because she was black, but swallowed her pride and chose to take the test again.

There seems to be some kind of awakening that takes place around this age. Girls are sensitive and vulnerable. Even if there are no major crises, the realization comes that it is possible to exert control, to make choices, and to take risks, but to do so courts disapproval.

Helene, our 1960s graduate, said that her parents did not want her to go to Hunter. "It meant traveling on the subway by myself. I was supposed to tell my school principal that my parents wouldn't let me go to take the test. Instead, I called my mother from school and said, "I'm going." I just insisted. In my eleven-year-old head I knew Hunter was hot stuff. My mother said, 'Well, if it means that much to you, go ahead.' I don't know where I got the chutzpah to defy my parents."

In her twenties, a young woman typically makes choices about a career, marriage, sexuality, more family decisions, pregnancy, and education. Kitty, class of '33, remembers that when she miscarried with her first child, she decided to quit working. "I wanted to have children, and there was the idea that you shouldn't work if you were pregnant. Afterwards, I chose to stay home with my children." Many women spoke of adjusting their work schedules in these years, and having to decide between staying home, part-time work, or full-time employment.

Renee, one of our 1950s graduates, remembered two critical choice points: "The first was marrying the person I chose to marry; and the other was divorcing him."

In her thirties, a woman often copes with choices about career advancement, divorce, money, relationships, pregnancy, and child-rearing.

In their forties and fifties, women often step back and reassess their lives. It's a time when many women seem to come face to face with a feeling of having been frozen in place. We frequently saw an alteration in course in the stories of women in this age group. The internal person fought to merge with the external circumstances she was in. Women spoke of trying to decide whether to go back to work or school, forge ahead on an established career, or change careers. They continued to walk a tightrope between taking care of themselves or extending themselves to others—but now leaned more towards self-preservation.

Roxanne, class of '43, retired from teaching in 1985 and enrolled in a training institute to become a therapist. "I had earned my Ph.D. several years earlier, and now I was ready for a complete career change. I feel for the first time my potential is being tapped.

Women are often late bloomers. But when they do bloom, they have solid achievements."

Kitty, who had stayed home with her family, went back to work when she was in her midforties. "That's when I got busy. I had a great job that eventually led to my becoming the head of the accounting department of a large corporation. I was a good executive."

In her older years, a woman continues to confront numerous choices. Will she choose independence over dependence, risk over security, activity over withdrawal? In this stage, too, there were many legitimate choices to be made.

GOVERNED BY EXPECTATIONS

Throughout these stages, we saw how in one powerful respect a woman's life passage is different from a man's. Throughout the twentieth century Hunter women had made choices shaped by the expectations and restrictions imposed by their families, school, and society at large. In their lives, they told us, societal and family expectations overshadowed personal ambitions. This was true in 1910 and remained true in 1990.

They made life choices primarily in two ways: either they followed a path clearly defined by their families or teachers; or when adult guidance was vague, as it often was, they "tripped" into life choices by accident. In the early decades, women were held back from professional careers, and in later decades they were swept forward. In every case, their choices—and their lives—were shaped by the social currents flowing around them.

Sharon, from the class of '73, a partner in a Washington, D.C., law firm, says she never questioned her family's expectations. "I went along the path I was expected to travel. I went to schools I would have expected to go to. It could have been Radcliffe instead of Princeton, Yale instead of Harvard for law school. The deviation would have been within a very narrow range. There were certain built-in expectations that are overriding. You never quite feel happy with yourself unless you fulfill them."

Rosemarie, a financial analyst from a very poor family, whose intelligence took her through Sarah Lawrence and, later, Wharton, feels that she never made conscious choices to pursue those academic and career roads. "I sort of tripped over things. I went away to college to get out of the house; I moved to Atlanta because I had a boyfriend there. I got a job in a bank because it was an easy thing to do. After a while, an M.B.A. seemed to make sense. It was sort of a series of nondecisions. They were never accompanied by a lot of major soul searching."

The reforming social currents of their times swept Sharon and Rosemarie along with them. Both have made successful professional careers that they find rewarding. Neither thought much about the course they set in life. In this, they were identical to their Hunter sisters of earlier generations who abided by the expectations of their times. Many described a vague, undefined method of making choices. Rosemarie's words "I tripped over it" was a theme repeated almost verbatim by other women in professional careers.

Helene described how she accidentally found her career path in city planning. "I was dating a guy who lived in a commune in Hoboken. One of the women was leaving the commune to go back to graduate school to study city planning. I asked her, 'What's city planning?' When she told me, I said, 'Oh, my God! Such a thing exists?' It all sort of clicked. I absolutely tripped over it."

This pattern of following expectations or stumbling along was so ingrained that when adult women came to a critical choice point they seemed unable or unwilling to get in touch with their own desires. They often looked around and waited for someone to choose for them. Many said they never saw the opportunity to choose and stumbled blindly across the choice point. "I don't know why I did that," they often said. Several women who tried to juggle working with child care and family life said, "I muddled my way through it."

There is no feminine gene that programs a woman to be vague

and uncertain about choices. Her vertigo comes from trying to walk a tightrope between her own desires and the needs and expectations of others.

A man also faces choice points, but he is better able to assess the options, and make his own decision. Among other things, he does not have to trade or postpone his career for fatherhood, or vice versa, and he benefits from the support of society's structure.

We saw how hard it was for a woman to make space for herself, to reach the inner self where she could make a free choice based on her own convictions. Sometimes, she made no choice at all and simply turned her back on the options. But as the contemporary theologian Harvey Cox has said, "Not to decide is to decide." Whether they faced it, denied it, were turned away by it, or let the critical choice point slide by, the moment directly affected the outcome of their lives.

Here, then, was a possible link to the missing excellence factor. At life's important turning points these women, no matter how smart they were, were held back—*or held themselves back*—from taking responsibility in directing their own lives.

Because they have few roles models and recognizable paths of opportunity, women who go against the grain and try to make their own choice may be unable to get a fix on their direction in life. Some of the women said that when they did choose to challenge the social system of their era there were often painful consequences. Their friends and family often disapproved of their choice, or they were ridiculed by colleagues. Some said their children resented them and, in more than one instance, marriages broke up.

FREEDOM TO CHOOSE

Career and personal choices made with self-awareness and freedom are "successful." Those made to satisfy someone else's needs or expectations are not, although they may outwardly appear to be. A woman who aims for the top ranks of the most competitive, male-dominated profession and the woman who teaches elementary school or stays home to raise her kids are equally successful—or equally unsuccessful—depending on the way she makes the choice, whether her own ambitions and dreams are an integral part of the process or she has acquiesced to another's wishes.

The Hunter study made it clear that for women to fulfill their promise they needed to develop and experience their freedom to choose and to risk the consequences.

FROZEN IN PLACE

Many Hunter women tried to rationalize their choices, and dedicated themselves compulsively to lesser tasks, while they secretly craved more. They tried to be perfect wives and mothers, or were pleased to climb only to the middle rung of the corporate ladder.

Accepting less than is possible guarantees freezing of growth and potential. Some of the common warning signs of a woman frozen in her tracks are:

- A sense of boredom and ennui
- Constant frustration and irritation
- Anger welling up, followed by sadness and remorse.

These feelings are characterized by their intensity and lack of focus. "You just feel mad at everybody and everything."

Many people often feel stuck in their lives, but a smart woman experiences her paralysis more acutely. In order to make her life work, she has denied her gifts and possibilities.

ACTIVE ENGAGEMENT

This very paralysis can be the forerunner of change. When a woman just can't stand it any more—when she is most irritated and fed up or tired of the way things are—that is when she can become aware of critical choice points. And it is then that she can begin to make choices, regardless of what anybody else says or thinks.

When we looked at the stories of the Hunter women we began to see how change might occur, despite society's unwillingness to open up the top rungs of power. As therapists, we have always encouraged women to act on their convictions and take responsibility for the choices they make and be vigilant of the consequences. And yet we realize how much more difficult this is for women to do than men.

We believe that if a woman will recognize the critical choice points of her life, she stands a greater chance of breaking through the social and familial prejudices that work against her. A choice clearly seen can become a momentous opportunity for growth.

A key ingredient of leadership is the willingness to take risks. Many Hunter women said they were extremely hesitant to take risks, and equated this fear with their inability to fulfill their potential. Most voiced the feelings of Kitty, class of '33: "I don't think I'm a risk-taker. I'm a plodder. I do the next step."

Surprisingly, women of two divergent decades—the 1960s and the 1910s—stood out as risk-takers, probably due to the large social and industrial movements of these decades. Both of these eras also were periods of great national danger, when the country was involved in World War I and Vietnam. The other decades were mainly devoid of women in our study who called themselves risk-takers.

Each choice point offers us a way to take risks, to make leaps and draw upon our deepest inner resources to develop our fullest potential. We have come to call this process Active Engagement, a process that embodies recognizing and acting on the choice points that occurs within the unique lives women lead. Active Engagement encourages women to make fully conscious choices for which they assume responsibility. In this way we believe women can more fully create their own lives, while meeting their sense of obligation to others.

From the more than forty Hunter women we personally interviewed, we have selected fifteen to represent the decades of this century. We chose women who have taken different life journeys, and sometimes, but not always, ended up in similar places. While their names, occupations, and exact year of graduation have been changed to protect their privacy, the facts are absolutely without embellishment or artifice. And although the stories of these fifteen women will make up the primary fabric of our tapestry, the voices and feelings of many others will be heard throughout, woven in and out for the fullest and most revealing picture.

Despite its public-school standing, the students of Hunter for most of this century were almost exclusively white, and dominated by middle- and upper-middle–class girls. Yet because students were culled from neighborhoods all over New York, in any given decade the student body also included girls of widely varying economic and ethnic backgrounds. The fifteen women we chose reflect that diversity. They are of Irish, German, Italian, and Greek descent. They are Catholic and Jewish and Protestant. Two are Afro-American. Four were raised by their single working mothers. Several of the older women were daughters of immigrant families. Two come from moneyed, highly educated families, eight from middle-class families, and five from economically disadvantaged backgrounds. By profession they are teachers, lawyers, executives, accountants, writers, psychotherapists, and public servants; the youngest is still trying to decide what to do.

THE WOMEN

REGINA, class of '14, was born into an upper-middle–class Victorian family in 1898. She graduated from Hunter in the middle of World War I. The war brought dramatic changes to Regina's life. She spent her early married years in Greenwich Village, soaking up the bohemian artist's life. Her husband died young, leaving her with three sons to support. She became an accomplished public speaker and journalist.

IRENE, class of '24, born in 1907, was eleven years old when World War I ended. Although she is only eight years younger than Regina, she came of age in a completely different atmosphere. Irene graduated from Hunter during the Roaring Twenties. Hers was a harshly deprived childhood, yet as an officer in the Foreign Service she became one of Hunter's most successful graduates. She never married and has no children.

KITTY, class of '33, was born in 1916 to immigrant Irish parents. She started elementary school at the beginning of the boisterous 1920s and was still in high school when the crash came in 1929. Her hopes for the future were drastically altered by the Depression. She became a bookkeeper, and raised two daughters.

ROXANNE, class of '43, was born in 1926. Growing up all through the Depression, she graduated from Hunter after the start of World War II. Her mother was a schoolteacher and her father a political activist. Roxanne is now a psychoanalyst, divorced from her husband after more than twenty years of marriage. She has one child.

INGRID, class of '53, RENEE, '57 and PHYLLIS, '58, were all born just before the beginning of World War II. Their parents had been desperately affected by the Depression, but their own childhoods coincided with the dislocation and upheaval of the war, and the subsequent economic revitalization. Their adolescence was later played out in the calm oblivion of the 1950s. From the late 1930s to the 1950s, the life of each was tempered·by these three vastly different decades. All three are married and have adult children. Ingrid became a classical scholar, Phyllis a dedicated teacher; Renee heads an advertising agency.

HELENE, class of '62, GRACE, '68, and ROSEMARIE, '69, were born during the postwar baby boom. Their childhood was in the 1950s, but their teenage years coincided with the social revolution of the 1960s. They had three different reactions to that movement: Helene, from a tightly knit Greek Sephardic family that disdained education, used the rallying cries of the 1960s to fight for her own independence. Grace comes from a family of scholars, and was the only one of five children to try to forge a career outside of academics; first as a singer, and now as a writer. Rosemarie was fast-tracked by her parents into law school and became one of the first female partners in a major international law firm.

EILEEN, class of '72, and SHARON, '73, were children in the late 1950s and 1960s, but reached maturity in the 1970s, as the hippie movement abated and Abbie Hoffman got a job. Each felt the impact of the women's movement in her life, and each achieved a successful, high-paying business career in the big-money decade of the 1980s. Sharon is unmarried; Eileen, after eleven years of marriage, has just had her first child.

LAUREN, class of '76, EMILY, '77, and JOYCE, '82, are among the youngest Hunter women interviewed. Lauren and Emily both come from wealthy families, with successful working parents. Both are married, and both are feeling the relentless pressure of demanding high-performance jobs, and wondering what the future holds for them. Joyce is still trying to find her "niche" in life.

By sharing their stories we hope to show how all women can become more fully aware of their own choices, freedom, promise, and power; how they can create and chart their own life courses and have a more profound and pervasive impact on the world—all the way to the top.

THREE

GROWING UP

A perfect little doll.
—PHYLLIS, *class of '58*

THE GOOD-GIRL SYNDROME

As we listened closely to the stories Hunter women told about their childhoods, we were struck by one resounding theme. Whether the woman was ninety or nineteen, whether she grew up in the Depression or in the 1950s, whether she was raised by one parent or two—almost to a woman, they shared one common trait: almost all said they were "good girls."

Sharon, the thirty-five-year-old lawyer, said, "I did the right thing. I knew what my parents wanted, and I did it. If anything, I felt like I should be doing more."

Ingrid, now in her late fifties, told us that she had made a lot of choices in her lifetime, "but they were all pretty much based on pleasing my parents. I was the best—the best daughter, the best senior class president, the best student."

Cynthia, now forty-one years old, said, "I would rail against the characterization of 'good girl,' but God knows, to a certain extent I probably was. Particularly when you think that I grew up in the

1960s, when you were supposed to misbehave. I never did. I was the child who reported to the class. Or the person who stood up and welcomed the parents when the mothers came. From Girl Scouts, from Brownies, from fourth grade, all my life. I wore white glvoes, because my mind was white gloves. There was a certain way that I expected myself to behave. I got a lot of approval for it."

Even the few Hunter women who said they were rebellious felt bad about not being "good." Regina, one of our oldest living graduates, said that her parents were astounded at her mild turn-of-the-century rebellion. "I was a very conforming and polite little girl. I respected my parents, obeyed our home rules, and rarely questioned what was asked of me. One evening, however, my father was reading and my brother, David, was doing his homework. I was helping my mother do the dishes. I remember standing at the kitchen sink, putting my hands on my hips, and demanding, "Why is David so special when it comes to doing dishes? Don't I count as much? What about me?

"In our household I was considered an impudent, nasty little girl for talking that way to my mother. It wasn't just my manner, it was that I dared to question the givens. Being rude and defiant, as my parents viewed it, deserved punishment and they delivered it. It wasn't anything physically abusive, but I was a sensitive child, so that even a scolding made me feel ashamed. Even though I didn't have to do the dishes anymore, I felt bad for being rude."

Joyce, who graduated from Hunter more than sixty years later, put it this way: "I was taught if you do good, good will come back to you. I'm just now finding out it may not be so."

Where does all this need for goodness come from? And what does this early labeling mean in the larger scheme of things?

When we casually asked fifty-one-year-old Phyllis if she had been a "good daughter," her eyes filled with tears. "I am so tormented by this that it is the strongest force in my life." Phyllis, ash blond hair carefully coiffed, presents herself with the erect posture and meticulous grooming she learned as a young woman in the

1950s. She is so composed that the trace of tears in the light hazel eyes surprises us. When I ask her to continue, she closes her eyes and hesitates.

"What do you think is going on?" I asked.

"My life is coming unglued. I'm working myself to death, and there's just no let-up. I work seventy to eighty hours a week writing grant proposals for my school, my husband decides to quit his job, my mother isn't speaking to me. Where do you want me to begin?"

"I seem to have struck a nerve."

"I guess you did."

Phyllis smiled, then backed up and started from the beginning: "I grew up in Washington Heights and what I remember most is the feeling of neighborhood. In those days the Heights was largely a Jewish immigrant neighborhood, with other ethnic groups mixed in. My father, Aaron, drove a taxi for a living, but he was really a very fine musician. For extra money he played the accordion and the violin at weddings and bar mitzvahs, and during the war he had a lot of extra work on the weekends. I don't know why he wasn't called for the draft. Afterwards, when the younger men came back from overseas, there were a lot more musicians competing for those jobs, and a lot more gasoline available, so he concentrated more on his taxi driving.

"My mother was a homemaker. She was very bright and capable, a very strong force, basically for the good, basically to encourage her children to achieve. My brother and I were both bright, and my mother was devoted to us."

Phyllis's parents, like other parents of bright children, were the first to recognize her daughter's special qualities. Her mother, Pearl, noticed that even as an infant Phyllis had a special alertness and curiosity about her environment, wanted to use all of her senses to reach out and decode her world. "My mother always said that my eyes were so big that they could take in more than other babies'." Like most bright children, Phyllis walked early, talked sooner than other children, and had a vocabulary as large as her brother's, who was two-and-a-half years older.

Pearl probably felt her own dreams had come true when she saw her daughter who was so quick and responsive, who delighted in learning and seemed so easily to achieve. It's not unusual for parents of bright daughters to begin to idealize their child, seeing the child as flawless and perfect. Pearl was no exception. "My mother always said I was a 'perfect little doll,' " Phyllis acknowledged.

Phyllis learned to read before she started school, and was able to grasp ideas and tell stories herself when she was still quite small. Like most smart little girls, she was also exceptionally intuitive in her response to adults, picking up even the most subtle cues to fit into the role assigned. As she achieved and performed for her parents, she fulfilled every facet of a "good girl."

After a brief period of babyhood, Phyllis appeared so capable that she was given adultlike tasks to perform. "My mother ran our house and everyone in it with the efficiency of a general. I don't know how my brother and father felt about the antiseptic atmosphere of our apartment, but even as a very small child I hated the constant cleaning it required. I learned everything about housekeeping, and everything had to be just so. My mother was a perfectionist. When we folded the laundry, the towels had to present the rounded edge forward. We ironed our underwear. Absolute precision about everything."

"What would happen if you made a mistake?" I asked.

"It depended on her mood. She could be wonderful about it, or she could turn cold. I remember offering to help her mop the kitchen floor one afternoon, and she grabbed my arm and said, 'You can help me most by staying out of my way.' I didn't know what I had done wrong."

Phyllis perceived her mother as the person with power in the family and the person she wanted to please most. She could share in this power by being like her mother and fulfilling her wishes. Pearl was clearly the major force in Phyllis's life, revolving prismlike in front of her daughter, one moment the charming, encouraging mother, the next a frustrated woman looking for fulfillment by the only means she had—controlling the behavior of those closest to her.

Phyllis became a master of sensing the moods and wishes of both her parents. "I was the peacemaker between my parents. My father adored my mother, but there was always an undercurrent of tension between them. My mother claimed his family rejected her, and he resented her comments. To make peace between them, I would sing with my father, and I would help my mother cook dinner. I tried to soothe them so they would relax."

But even Phyllis, the perfect child, had her limits. Phyllis said she remembered V-E Day, in May 1945, as if it were yesterday, because it marked a significant change in her life.

"It was a cold, sunny day and everyone was out in the streets. The end of the war in Europe meant so much to us, it was such a tremendous tide of relief and gladness. I was about six years old, and all of us neighborhood kids formed a column and marched up and down the sidewalks, waving little American flags. Then we got to running and screaming and working ourselves up into the general mood of rejoicing. The wind was whipping up the streets, and suddenly I couldn't catch my breath. I started to gasp and fell down on the sidewalk. My brother was jeering me, but when he saw the panic on my face he ran for my mother. I'll never forget my mother lifting me up in her arms. I was still clutching my flag, because I had the idea I was supposed to keep it from falling to the ground. That was the first time I had an asthma attack."

From that time on, whenever she would physically overexert herself Phyllis would have an asthma attack. "Sometimes I would have to rest in bed for weeks. I remember these times with pleasure, actually, because my mother was so loving. I would sit up in bed and draw and she would tell me stories or read to me. She was a wonderful companion when I was sick. Even though I had this breathing problem, she always encouraged me to do everything that I wanted. She scrimped and saved to give me music lessons and art lessons. I always wanted to dance, but that was the one thing I wasn't permitted because I would have a wheezing attack. I left the dancing to my mother. My father always said mother was the best dancer he had ever seen."

Phyllis's poor health gave her a break from the stresses of high performance and also protected her from having to compete directly with her mother. When she was sick, she had a chance to be a baby. When she was well, she performed at top speed.

COVER-UP AND AVOIDANCE

Smart girls quickly learn that their accomplishments may not be an asset outside the home. Phyllis said that her elementary school classmates didn't think she was so special. "Certainly, no one fussed over me the way my mother did. The worst thing you could be at school was different. And I had a reputation of being sort of an oddball, and I felt very timid around other kids. I got teased a lot because of my asthma and because my mom gave me these elaborate Shirley Temple–type hairdos."

Another Hunter woman also remembered being teased by children in elementary school, and that was over a decade after Phyllis's time. Rosemarie said, "The kids in school tormented me because I was smart. When I took the test for Hunter I got the highest score, and the other kids in my school made fun of me. I was so relieved to get away from them."

To cope with the envy and rejection that often accompanies their success, smart girls may try to cover up their abilities. Some deliberately postpone their responses to teacher's questions to give others a chance. Others, comfortable with adults, form an alliance with their teachers. Phyllis fell into this category. "I always tried to please the teacher. If we had a class outing, I would always try to walk with the teacher and ingratiate myself. I remember one first-grade outing to a museum where they had a mummy on display. I told my teacher I wanted to be an archaeologist when I grew up.

She was very impressed that I knew what an archaeologist was."

The idea of the child hiding her real self inside—and trotting out the pretend self to satisfy the wishes and demands of adults— is a common theme among smart girls. A child like Phyllis, so expert at pleasing others, eventually loses touch with her own true self.

A crisis loomed in the family as Phyllis began to mature. "When I was about ten, my hair started to change color from a reddish gold that my mother adored, and grow dark. My mother wanted to bleach it, but my father wouldn't let her. Also, the secret about my eyesight got out. I had never been able to see well, but I was afraid to tell anyone, for fear I would have to wear glasses. My mother always boasted about my beautiful green eyes. In school, when we had our vision tested, everyone stood in line and when your turn came, you stepped forward and read the eye chart. From the time I was about five or six I would listen to the child ahead of me and, when my turn came, I'd repeat what she had read. I got away with it until I was eleven, when they started testing us in a separate room. From then on, I had to wear glasses."

Phyllis's mother saw the physical changes in her "little doll" and didn't like what she saw. "Here I was, big, not tiny as I had been. I was almost fully grown by the time I was twelve. I wasn't pretty anymore, although my mother never said so. I wore glasses, and my hair was a kind of mousy brown."

Adolescence is a watershed for bright girls. Separating from parents is seen as the critical task of adolescence for both girls and boys, but separation can be painful for good girls who have learned to please their parents at all costs. By definition separating means rejecting, or at least reassessing, parental values. Adolescence is a time of painful self-differentiation, a time when family is cast aside and an identity is formed that is the individual's alone. A daughter normally vacillates between disregard for her parents and idealiza- tion of them. Her mother is, at this juncture, both her competitor and her role model. To increase her own esteem and measure her effectiveness as a woman, a daughter usually needs to diminish her mother for a time.

Phyllis sidestepped the issue completely. She neither confronted her parents nor rebelled against their values. She kept herself to herself. She was expert at this, because she had been doing it since childhood.

At Hunter, Phyllis finally began to develop her own identity. "All kinds of girls went there," she recalled. "Suddenly, *everybody* wasn't Jewish. Yes, there was snobbishness, but I was artistic, and that cuts through a lot of layers. I was a good singer and actress, always ready and eager to be in the plays and sings and things. You're accepted everywhere if you're talented and show it off. Everything just opened up for me."

Phyllis described Hunter as the "cornerstone" of her inner life. She said that for the first time she shared her real self—her own feelings and opinions—with her peers. "That was the best part. Although, because we were all overachievers, I had to push myself even more to the limits of perfection."

The Hunter women had an advantage over other teenage girls because they were expected to compete with other smart girls, and thus they avoided one of the common hazards of adolescence. According to studies by Harvard professor Carol Gilligan, the teenage years are often the time when a girl begins to deny her brain power and bow to the pressure to conform to a lower standard of achievement. Even if a girl has managed to hang on to a strong self-image in childhood, she is now subject to powerful pressures to fit in with a peer group that often judges girls solely in terms of physical attractiveness.

If an adolescent girl begins to dilute her achievements in order to become part of the crowd, it is a daily insult to her self-esteem. She begins a journey towards self-betrayal. The moment she begins to give up her authentic feelings, her ability to achieve is blocked.

Many Hunter women said they were able to avoid this trap.

Cynthia, class of '67, said, "Nobody had ever told me that I had to be subservient, that I had to pretend that I was stupid in order to attact a boy's attention. As a matter of fact, between seventh and twelfth grades I hardly knew any boys."

Most agreed with her, although several admitted that outside of school they were subtly encouraged to cover up their brightness. Christine, class of '57, said, "I knew I shouldn't win all the time, or even most of the time. My mom would tell me, 'Give someone else a chance, dear.' She meant 'Let them win.' "

Several Hunter women said that they lived two different lives. At Hunter they were usually encouraged to be smart, to speak out, to think, and to argue. At home, they were encouraged to be good and conforming. Even though their parents often appreciated their gifts, they stopped short of encouraging their daughters to be different from other children or different from other members of the family.

As Phyllis matured, Pearl seemed to vacillate between pride and competitiveness with her daughter—creating a grandiose fantasy of Phyllis's gifts one minute, and forcing her into relinquishing them the next.

Like a number of women who came of age in the late 1950s, Phyllis was brought up to believe that she would raise a family and she would also have a profession. "I knew I was not supposed to be a satellite person of a man. I felt constantly that to please my mother I would have to do the things that she did—run a household and everyone in it—and also have a career."

Pearl set her eyes toward the future and began to shape Phyllis into the adult she herself would like to have been. To whatever extent some mothers have suppressed their own longings, to that same degree will their daughters be pressured to fulfill them. The pressure inevitably creates a conflict for the daughter. Phyllis was caught in a bind: succeed to please Pearl, but do not outstrip her.

Pearl had wanted to be a schoolteacher, and now she laid that dream out for Phyllis. "My mother had dropped out of college because she had no money. She worked two jobs and turned over her paychecks to her parents. They sent her brother to college instead. My mother never got over it."

Pearl, at least on the surface, accepted the norms of her time. She married and devoted herself to her family. "Relegating my mother to care for two kids and a four-room apartment was like using a nuclear reactor to run a toaster. She was so capable and efficient, she could have run the world. As it was, she ran us.

"Early on, my mother decided that my brother, Larry, would be a doctor and I would be a teacher. There's no question that my parents had higher aspirations for Larry than for me. In her mind, becoming a teacher was a great thing for a girl."

I asked Phyllis whether she felt her mother was competitive with her, or if her conservative ambitions for her daughter merely reflected the attitudes of the 1950s.

"I'm not certain what her feeling was. I think she probably underappreciated my abilities. But, really, people didn't have high aspirations for girls in those days."

Other women of various decades were equally confused about their mother's feelings toward their abilities. Most seemed to think the era dictated the attitude. Regina remembered that in the Victorian age, "people didn't try to understand their children. Nobody ever asked, 'How do you feel?' or 'Do you like your school?' or 'What do you think of the book you're reading?' Certainly not of little girls."

Eighty years later, in a supposedly more enlightened era, Toni's mother, a successful career woman, told Toni that if she expected to have a good life she had better nab a rich husband. Even now, she could say to her smart daughter, "You're bright and capable, but look for a wealthy man to support you." Toni, class of '86, said, "I don't really believe that I'm smart, but my mother's probably right about marrying rich. I don't know how I could earn a lot of money."

Phyllis said, finally, "I guess it's a little bit of both—it was clear that I was supposed to live out my mother's dreams, which were fairly limited, but I wasn't supposed to go beyond them. Was that competition? Or did she just not have any markers for me to follow?"

Either way, for a clever child who had learned to sidestep confrontation and meet the needs of adults, choosing a profession was going to present problems. Phyllis faced this significant choice point when she was in her late teens.

Throughout her growing-up years, Phyllis was well recognized for creative talents in high school. "I wanted to be an actress like Uta Hagen. I wanted to be a writer like Lillian Hellman. I looked at everything through an artist's eyes. I was president of the drama club at Hunter. I loved playmaking. And I was a pretty good painter. I thought there was a place waiting for me in American theater. My friends and teachers at school all expected me to have a fabulous career in the arts, most likely the theater."

When it came time for college, money loomed as a huge factor in Phyllis's future. "My parents assumed I would go on to Hunter College because it was free. It took every penny they had to send my brother through medical school, so there definitely wasn't any money for me.

"But Hunter College was not known for its creative arts programs. At *my* insistence, the guidance office at Hunter processed my application to two private colleges. I was accepted at both, but chose New York University because it offered the biggest scholarship."

For Phyllis to have graduated from Hunter High with a full scholarship in fine arts to New York University meant that she must have been at the top of her graduating class, which in Hunter terms means the brightest of the bright. "My parents didn't know what to think, but they couldn't argue with it. Everything was paid for and, suddenly, for the first time in my life I felt free.

"But as soon as I arrived on campus, I got cold feet. I knew that studying the arts wasn't going to put food on the table. It was as if my parents' voices were ringing in my ears. I figured I'd better do something that would guarantee me some kind of a job when I got out."

Phyllis then selected courses from education *and* theater arts. "I marched up the steps to the dean and explained my plan to him. He permitted me to transfer my scholarship to the school of education and liberal arts at the same time. I've been sailing on two ships ever since." By doubling her major to include both teaching and art, Phyllis seemed to fill her parents' expectations without completely abandoning her own dreams.

"I felt relieved; I knew my mother would be happier. Yet at the same time I felt a twinge of disappointment." That "twinge" was the emergence of her inner self, the one being forced to recede again. We have all made choices like this many times, sometimes in small, seemingly insignificant ways. The important signal is the immediate sense of disappointment blinking like a red light. Several of our women spoke of letting their dreams go in youth. Ingrid said, "I can remember the look on my professor's face when I said I was going to get married instead of taking up a scholarship to Oxford. It shot through me like a current."

In her senior year Phyllis married, and later juggled teaching with raising two children. She turned down job opportunities to enter radio and television broadcasting and went on to develop arts programs in the public school system.

Not all Hunter women accepted without argument the persona demanded by their mothers. Some women tried to be different, but not so different that they courted social disapproval. Some initially rebelled, then returned to the roles encouraged by their mothers.

In the 1940s, Renee's mother was a hugely successful career woman, a pioneer in the advertising business. "She was like Rosalind Russell in the movies," Renee says. "My immediate inclination was to avoid following in her footsteps. Although I didn't want to be a traditional housewife and mother, I also did not want to duplicate my mother's life—which is ironic, because today, at age fifty-one, I'm the CEO of an advertising agency. A funny trick got played on me."

A few daughters fully opposed what had been modeled for

them, either with polite refusal to conform or in open rebellion. The Hunter women reported their fair share of emotional break-downs and psychotherapy in their teens. Teri, class of '76, said she "completely flipped out." She eventually moved all the way across the country to San Diego and took up herbal healing, in direct defiance of her scholarly family of doctors. Nevertheless, she still pursued a career in the health profession.

Phyllis remembers the stages of her young adult life in her twenties and thirties as a good and fulfilling time. Her teaching work was rewarding, she enjoyed her children, and her parents fully approved of the way she lived her life. After a while, however, her level of satisfction diminished. Phyllis wanted more, but she felt it was too late to pursue a theatrical career. Instead, in 1963, she went back to school and earned a master's and then a Ph.D. in education. Getting a Ph.D. was an "acceptable" way for Phyllis to go beyond Pearl, without incurring her mother's outright wrath. Predictably, Pearl disapproved. Phyllis had gone far enough, she said, why did she need to take valuable time away from her family? However, aside from an occasional dig—"You're always finding another project to keep yourself too busy"—Pearl let it ride. After all, Phyllis was still vaguely within acceptable bounds.

Today, Phyllis is dedicated to her work, and finds it rewarding much of the time. But she is aware that she has chosen another safe path. "My work is a socially acceptable form of the arts, without my really being an 'artist.' It's very conforming."

One of Phyllis's problems, as she sees it today, is how little recognition she receives for her efforts. "Right now, I'm working at about four different jobs, writing massive grant proposals to fund these arts programs. I'm working all the time, night and day. To be quite honest, I would like to have some additional input financially from my husband. But he has chosen to occupy himself with his own interests, writing a novel."

PERFECTIONISM

We heard about many different kinds of growing up from the Hunter women. Certain common themes emerged: early recognition of a child's abilities, a push to excel, and a strong tendency toward perfectionism.

It's difficult for parents of smart girls to accept that there may be some areas where even the brightest, most talented child may be less capable. If she has been primed to believe that she must be outstanding in everything, she may be unable to tolerate being less than perfect in some things.

Children often expect so much of themselves that they become perfectionists. We saw this tendency in many of the Hunter women. Frightened that they might not live up to the idealized vision of themselves, they withdrew from taking risks that might expose imperfections. Phyllis put it this way: "What I've lacked all my life is the ability to take risks, to pursue something within which there is danger of failure. I want to be free from that perfection compulsion that takes joy out of experiences."

One of the themes we heard repeatedly from the Hunter women was they only wanted to try things where they *knew* they could succeed. Twenty-six-year-old Joyce spoke for many Hunter women when she said, "If I know I can do something, then I'm totally confident and courageous. I can fly. But if I'm not sure, I hold back."

CONFORMITY

Some girls feel guilty when they are told that they are good, because they really resent obeying their parents. They feel their parents aren't seeing their true selves. Some daughters misbehave to show their parents how they really feel; more often, they withdraw and keep their angry and aggressive thoughts to themselves. This pattern dovetails with the "good-girl syndrome," where the real self is kept secret. "My parents had absolutely no sense of who I was," said Phyllis. "I was inside looking out, but they didn't see me."

Roxanne, who graduated in 1943, fifteen years earlier than Phyllis, also conformed to her mother's wishes, although she remembered that her mother held few expectations for her. "Teenagers really didn't defy their parents then. If anything, you put up a good front, and if you had a problem you tried to solve it without letting your mother know. My mother was an elementary school teacher, which was okay for a mother to be in the 1940s. Despite the fact that she earned our daily bread, she idealized males. If one sex is wonderful, then the other sex has to take second place. My mother took for granted I would do well in school, but I don't think she had any real dreams for me. After college, I wanted to teach on the university level. My mother said there weren't jobs for women in colleges. I applied, but was told that I didn't need the job as much as a male who would head a household. So I meekly lowered my expectations for myself and taught elementary school like my mother. I think now I was afraid to surpass her."

In the 1960s, Helene's mother had conflicting feelings about her daughter's intelligence and success in school, but Helene rebelled. "My mother was very torn when she saw I was a bright little girl. My family were working-class Greek immigrants, Sephardic Jews, where traditional roles for women held sway. My mother was the first in her family to graduate from high school. She was a smart woman herself, but if she ever harbored dreams outside of family life, she never said so. Then I came along. The more I wanted to participate in the world, the harder it was for her to deal with me. She thought I should be a secretary."

Roxanne in the 1940s, Helene in the 1960s, and Phyllis caught in between—their common theme links many of the Hunter women. Their parents wanted the best for them, but often failed to recognize and encourage their tremendous potential.

FATHERS AND DAUGHTERS

Hunter women spoke mostly of their mothers when describing their struggles to free themselves from the shadows of their families and establish their own identities. Normal development for a girl implies identification with her mother, whose way of being invites the child to become a woman. Fathers, on the other hand, had an often unrecognized impact on the development of their daughters' lives. Hunter women tended to describe their fathers in three major ways: the patriarch, or benevolent dictator, who ruled and often oppressed; the absent father; and, occasionally, the nurturing, admiring supporter.

The patriarch was often idealized and described by our pre-1960s women as the wise ruler, the one who made decisions for everyone. He was stern, fair, strong, and protective. He encouraged respect and discouraged independence. Because his children weren't allowed to make their own decisions, in adult life they continued to rely on "father figures"—husbands, presidents, supervisors, and clergy. These daughters had trouble becoming their own guides and usually could not see themselves as capable of leading others.

Many Hunter women, including Irene, Ingrid, Joyce, and Rosemarie, had lost their fathers when they were young, usually through divorce or abandonment. Whether he was physically absent from the home or just emotionally detached, the absent father communicated an indifference to his child.

The daughter without a father may feel that her accomplishments are not worth much. She may give up early, or may try harder and harder to impress him, even in her imagination. This type of fathering, or lack of it, is the most difficult for the child to bear because she has no real idea of what a man is like. She lives on father fantasies. She must imagine the relationship and create reasons why her father left her and her mother. A daughter abandoned by her father may have to fight throughout her life to overcome feelings of guilt and inadequacy. Way down deep, the child blames herself, or her mother, for her father's departure and sees the father as a blameless victim. If she were better, prettier, *something*, he would have stayed.

Christine, class of '57, clearly described her feelings about her father, who abandoned her when she was three years old. "I have *never* been able to feel anger toward my father. My mother was mad enough for both of us. I adored my father and can remember sitting all day and night on my birthday or on Christmas Eve waiting for him to come to see me. He never did. This is so pathetic, but I never blamed him."

Joyce's father moved out when she was ten years old. For a few years afterward he came to see her on her birthday, then eventually stopped visiting her altogether. Unlike Christine, Joyce denies any feeling of loss. "He wasn't very important in my growing up," she said. "If I met him now, would I want it? It might just be too risky. If you knew what was inside Pandora's box, would you want to open it?"

Abandoned by her father, Joyce was carefully protected by her mother, who recognized and nurtured her daughter's unusual gifts. "As a child my mother had been farmed out to an aunt and never forgot how rejected she felt. She made up for it with me—she did everything for me." Recently, Joyce's mother retired from her job and moved to Atlanta. Without her mother, Joyce feels abandoned once more. "In its 'wonderfulness,' I suppose my mother's nurturing hindered my independence. I cannot seem to do the simplest things for myself. I've got to figure out how to feed the cat, go to the store, and get to work on time. All summer before my mother left I was running around with my friends pretending she wasn't going. Now, she's gone and I feel lost."

APPROVING FATHERS

As more women participate in the work force, some of their partners have begun to participate in the "home force," engaging in the daily tasks of parenting. Many men who have never known a nurturing father themselves find it difficult to know how to care for and support their children, particularly their daughters. However, there are those who seem to have accomplished this task. They have recognized the consequences of the lack of warmth and intimacy from their own fathers and have found ways to parent their children differently. The approving father acts as a renewable spring from which the child may drink, providing a source of confidence and assurance. If a male has been socialized to confront and challenge others, to test but not destroy his opponent, to realize that even if he fails he will still be worthy, he may be able to pass on to his daughter valuable lessons about the worthiness of leadership.

Robin, class of '83, recalls her relationship with a father who had little education himself, but encouraged his daughter to excel. "He was this funny mixture of Archie Bunker and Alistair Cooke. This redneck guy, my father, full of all these prejudices and attitudes, would ask me every night to read him my homework! Can you imagine? This ninth grade kid reading *Macbeth* to her father at the kitchen table over Pabst Blue Ribbon? But, he loved it, and I knew why. He was getting a glimpse of the education he had missed."

Long before men were encouraged to be more "feminine," Regina, class of 1914, enjoyed a father who encouraged and guided her development. She remembers that he read to her every night as a child, a special time for the two of them. And later, "When I entered my teens, my father generously offered me a free choice of anything I wanted. I didn't even consider frivolities of jewelry or clothes. Unhesitatingly, I asked for the writings of a man who died the year I marched in the first suffrage parade down Fifth Avenue! My father spent $50.00 for *The Complete Works of Mark Twain*— a huge sum in those days! The best present I could have gotten!"

And Martha, class of 1957, recalls the critical influence of her father in her decision to attend college. "I had worked all summer to save up enough money to attend college, but I knew deep down that there wasn't enough money to pay for tuition and books and all the other expenses. Finally, in August, my mother and father and I sat down together to add up our resources. The money just wasn't there, we all could see it. Finally, my father looked up and said, 'Marty, you're going,' and closed the account book. My mother and I both asked how and challenged him to answer. All he said was, 'I don't know, but I'll find a way.' And he did."

GRANDMOTHERS: THE FORGOTTEN FORCE

There are other close influences that can help shape a woman's future. It is often easier to identify the full impact of parental influences if you look back one more generation.

Several women told us their grandmothers provided more stability and nurturing then their parents. Roxanne, a 1943 graduate, had grown up in the 1930s, when there was a tremendous growth in the union movements, and when joining the Communist party was considered a respectable thing for a good union man to do. "My father actually traveled to the Soviet Union for a visit, and while he was gone my grandmother came to live with us. She was indulging and loving, stuffing me with all kinds of goodies, like grandmothers do. She said, 'I love you more than I love myself.' I didn't understand that because I didn't love myself."

Roxanne recalled that her grandmother was instrumental in choosing her career course. "Grandmother insisted that I become a teacher, which I did, because it was a secure profession. She wielded a lot of influence with my mother, and between them I was going to become a teacher. I don't recall ever thinking about what I might want to do."

The grandparents of several women in our study were immigrants who had a reverent attitude toward learning and the free education America guaranteed its citizens. One graduate remembers, "My grandmother used to pay me a penny every night to read my lessons out loud to her. She didn't understand a word of English."

Helene said that as an activist in the 1960s she got her political awareness from her grandmother. "My grandmother never learned to read, neither in Greek nor in English. She was the wisest person I've ever known in my life. She was also more broad-minded than anybody else in the family, including her own children.

"My own parents were nonpolitical. They thought you should follow the rules and everything would turn out okay. But my grandmother had a larger perspective."

Renee said her grandmother was determined to establish a line of female achievers. "My grandmother came over here from Russia at the age of seventeen, and she was determined to make a family that would fit into the American mainstream. She put all of her enormous drive into raising her children so that they valued success and achievement. My mother was the one who fulfilled that dream for her."

The family relationships of the Hunter women are too diverse to make any concrete analysis of the relay from grandmother to mother to daughter, except to say that in unique ways the life journey of every woman helps shape the lives of her female descendants. And that it is nourishing for women of the present to look back at the legacies from the past.

HOW TO HELP

Although the repercussions may not be seen until adult life, the roots of the missing excellence factor must lie in a woman's childhood, the greenhouse in which the seedpods of leadership form. Young females need help to recognize their own talents and abilities. They need someone to help them set challenging goals. Someone who encourages them to take risks, to begin, even as children, to aim high, strive for honors and awards, and learn the skills of leadership.

Not all smart females suffer the consequences of losing "self." Some are strong enough or lucky enough to make their own decisions, come what may. Children who go their own way may appear on the surface to be extremely selfish. They may turn inward and become secretive, trying to hibernate until childhood has run its course. They are sometimes angry and rebellious.

Those smart girls who escape, or overcome, the tyranny of perfection seem more willing to take risks as adults and thus put themselves in the position to achieve leadership.

Although many of the Hunter women had stable, loving parents, usually their parents articulated only the vaguest career goals for their daughters. As little girls they had rapidly grasped how society frowns upon anger in women, ridicules audacious, independent thinking, and rejects bold and controversial actions. Even very young females are smart enough to know that severe consequences can follow if they deviate from what is expected.

In his classic study, Terman described three traits that marked gifted students who later went on to achieve goals commensurate with their abilities: persistence, self-confidence, and lives well integrated with their professional goals.

A daughter's emotional development is largely set before she reaches school. It's imperative that parents know how to encourage and prepare their daughters for leadership in early childhood. Parents can help daughters identify their own goals and learn to make their own choices. They can provide encouragement and support that will help them withstand the inevitable setbacks that accompany ambition. When she falls short of "perfection" or makes mistakes, parents can give her the confidence to accept failure and move forward. Parents can also discuss conflicts their daughter feels about achievement versus social acceptance, about the price she may have to pay if she chooses to pursue an unconventional path, about how to make choices for herself.

For parents, the critical ingredient in parenting daughters who will grow into confident and risk-taking adults is demonstrating these same behaviors in the family. Parents can encourage bright daughters by stretching boundaries in their own lives. It's this attitude toward life—a willingness to risk and challenge limitations—that a daughter learns from her parents and other adults.

COMING TO GRIPS WITH CHILDHOOD

Women in their twenties have the advantage of youth to make changes to boost themselves into leadership ranks. They have the added benefit of growing up in a time when society has opened new pathways for women. They may be the daughters best able to make their own choices. That they still must struggle to do so comes as a surprise to many of them.

Joyce, for instance, our sheltered, talented 1980s graduate, has both the brains and the education to achieve much of what she desires. She has had a loving mother who supported and nourished her every step of the way. Yet she feels lost and directionless. Joyce also faces two tremendous challenges which could keep her from fulfilling her potential. She is black, which she knows is a disadvantage in many situations. And she has been, by her own description, overprotected, which has left her feeling dependent and somewhat incompetent.

To recapture the inner self, young women must tackle three tasks: identify the limiting factors in their childhood that might hamper future choices; separate from their parents and become responsible individuals; strengthen the true self by developing their own values. These three tasks are all interconnected and are usually accomplished together.

Smart women can move beyond the constraints of childhood and gain the courage to seek excellence. As Columbia University professor and noted author Carolyn G. Heilbrun says, "One can act, sometimes shocking oneself at one's courage or audacity. One lives with the terror, the knowledge of mixed motives and fundamental conflicts, the guilt—but one acts."

• FOUR •

WITHIN THE WALLS OF HUNTER

My teachers seemed to be on a holy mission

— *IRENE, class of '24*

Thomas Hunter, an Irish immigrant, founded Hunter High School in 1870, his mission then to create an environment where intellect and knowledge could flourish among women regardless of race, creed, or economic status. From the beginning, the school offered a rich culture for bright girls from all over New York City who had completed their eighth-grade courses and passed a special entrance exam. As Irene, now in her eighties, recalls, "Getting into Hunter was the best stroke of luck I ever had. At last, I had some reason to believe in myself and my future."

Irene's passage into Hunter was a far simpler one than that faced by her intellectual descendants over a half century later. In the intervening period, as the number of applicants swelled, the admissions policy changed, requiring not only good elementary school grades, but top scores on a standardized IQ test. In 1955, the label "school for the gifted" was officially applied by the Board of Education. To take the Hunter exam, applicants now had to have an IQ of 130 or higher, an "excellent grade school record," and a personal recommendation from their elementary or junior high school principal. The Hunter exam itself became even more rigorous.

Today, IQ tests are no longer required. However, a similar entrance test is still used: a two-part multiple choice test in mathematics and English, for a total of 150 points (each part is given equal weight). In addition, applicants are asked to write a short essay, which is judged on grammer and creativity. The essays of only the highest-ranking candidates are read, and students must score above 75 on the essay to be admitted. In 1965, Hunter began a program to promote entrance of talented students from disadvantaged backgrounds. The test scores required of these students (about thirty are admitted each year) are a scant few points lower.

By passing the academic hurdles of their decade, the girls who entered Hunter found a place that would nurture and foster their talents.

HUNTER AS REFUGE

Irene remembers that before she became a Hunter girl her life had been a series of misfortunes, beginning with the death of her mother when she was eight years old. "She was only twenty-nine years old. My mother was a violinist and my father was a painter. We lived in what they called genteel artistic poverty. My mother was the center of our lives. My father was like another child in the family. Mother loved and nurtured him, too, as she did us. When she died, I think we all lost our place in the world.

"My father turned inward. He was a brilliant and talented painter, but not much of a father. My little brother, George, and I clung to each other. Father made sure we had a roof over our heads, but then forgot we were there.

"After school I would spend time in my father's studio where I sat silently, watching him paint, hour upon hour. One day when I was in high school, I went into his studio and shuffled around a bit more than usual. He noticed me, stopped working, looked over his glasses, and said, 'Irene, what do you do now?' And I said, 'Oh, I go to high school, Hunter High School.' He just nodded and went back to his painting."

How can a child survive such harsh rejection and grow up to fulfill her potential? Many studies have shown that parental indifference can be far more damaging to a child's self-image than criticism, blame, or even abuse. Yet Irene had become one of Hunter's most accomplished and successful graduates. How had she managed to do this?

"Hunter was my salvation," she said. "I found a real home in those classrooms."

In the early decades of this century, Hunter High offered, according to Irene, a basic classical curriculum: four years of Latin, four years of English, three of history, two of science and math, one year of biology and zoology, three years of German or French, plus one year of art and public speaking. The limited athletics program included basketball in the school gymnasium and hockey on the field at 106th Street in Central Park.

Irene thrived on the curriculum, but said that socially she always felt like an outsider. She had been a reclusive child, and she described herself as painfully shy. Her loneliness was reinforced by her poverty. Irene was one of the girls who had to work outside of school to provide for basic needs.

The fragmented, stressful life Irene was leading drove her to the edge of despair. "When I was sixteen, I was so despondent about my life that I considered suicide. I had no family, really, no one to talk to. All I seemed to do was work, work, work. I think I just got tired and scared that that was all there would ever be. For a few awful days, killing myself seemed like a good way to end my troubles. I don't know what pulled me out of that slough, but I remember the despair vividly."

The fact that Irene so clearly remembers this period in her youth suggests that she came through a perilous crisis. She had lost not only her mother, but in a real sense her father, too. Overworked and overtired, she drove herself to achieve academically as a way of personal salvation, and worked nights to pay for her food and clothing. A skilled counselor might easily have recognized some of the danger signs in Irene's situation and been able to help her through this difficult period, but Hunter had no counselors in those days. Even later, after counselors were added to the staff, students said they were expected to solve their own problems. Hunter was then, and has continued to be, a place where learning comes before anything else.

As it was, Irene's teachers probably saved her life. Although they overlooked her emotional plight—possibly because she kept her troubles to herself or because they felt helpless to address the situation—they admired her gifts and encouraged her to develop her talents to their fullest. With their help, she was able to hold on to life until this desperate time passed.

"My teachers personified the spirit of the times, which vibrated with hope," Irene recalled. "Millions of poor, uneducated people had immigrated to America right after the turn of the century; then the First World War seemed to democratize the different classes of Americans. The promise was such that you could feel it with your hand. A better time was coming.

"My teachers seemed to be on a holy mission. My English teacher planted the concept that advanced education was the road to freedom of choice. I figured that the best way to escape from a hard, grinding life was to emulate her. She was a tremendous influence on me. She showed me how to *be*. I would watch her, just to see how she handled herself in front of the class, how she talked to people."

Walking in the footsteps of her teacher, Irene entered Hunter College as an education and English major. Training teachers was the mission of Hunter from its beginning, when the campus was named Female Normal and High School; in 1914, the college and high school were separated and renamed after Dr. Hunter. Although Hunter College was no longer limited to turning out female schoolteachers, the tradition persisted well into the 1960s, mirroring the larger culture.

Irene relates: "I graduated from Hunter College in 1928. I was lucky to grow up in a period when so much education was free, so many teachers were enthusiastic and caring for their students. The society seemed to overflow with opportunities, and I grasped them for myself. Education became the prime focus in my life. It was literally the difference between life and death."

Just as Irene was ready to face the world with her teaching certificate, new-found confidence and flags flying, life became hard again: "The Depression fell on us like a black shroud. I was fortunate enough to have landed a job before the crash, and I held on to it." Irene turned once more to the lifeline that had saved her before— education: "I taught during the day and went to graduate school at night." In the depths of the Depression, Irene earned a master's in education, a doctorate in English research at Columbia, and later a second master's degree in social work. Her remarkable education set the stage for her future:

"When World War Two started in Europe, recruiters were scouring college campuses for men and women qualified to join the various intelligence-gathering corps. They took one look at my Ph.D. and the three languages I spoke, and the next thing I knew I was working for the Office of Strategic Services in England. This was the opportunity I had been waiting for."

Irene's Ph.D. and language skills were hard to ignore. She made an effort to make herself engaging and was rewarded with a job in strategy and analysis.

At the end of the war Irene was invited to join the Foreign Service and participated in the founding of UNESCO. In the 1950s, she was appointed director of the United Nations High Commission for Refugees in Tunisia. Her mettle was tested when, as an officer for the United Nations, Irene faced intimidation and threats from her professional colleagues. When she first arrived in Tunis, as director of the Algerian Refugee Camps, the attaché who greeted her suggested that for her own good she should "get the hell out of here."

She was uncertain what to do until the next day, when the

American ambassador invited her to a small dinner party. "When I arrived" she remembered, "the room was filled with high-ranking officials. They impressed upon me that I was on a U.N. passport. If I got into any trouble with either the French or the Algerians, I was on my own. At the end of the evening, the ambassador shook my hand and said, 'Well, Irene, I'll give you two weeks.' "

Irene smiled remembering this story. "I stayed two years. I was the girl who had worked in a laundry to go to school; no one was going to chase me out of Tunisia. When I came home, I received a special commendation from Washington."

After her stint with the U.N., Irene went back to teaching. When we asked how she had balanced her professional life with her personal life, Irene said that an ambitious woman in her day usually chose between work and family. "The few professional women who were my contemporaries usually didn't combine both, with the exception of Eleanor Roosevelt. I don't know how women do it today.

"I don't think I could have worked and achieved a Ph.D. and done all the other things I did if I had had a family. But that wasn't a conscious decision on my part. I've just never found time to marry, but my relationships with men have been very satisfactory, except, of course, with my father. I've been lucky, since I've met and worked with very bright men. I haven't missed that part of it. But I wish I'd had children. I've always wanted to have a family, but it just didn't work out."

Irene has little time for regrets. "I'm currently working on a directory of services for the homeless in my Upper East Side neighborhood. Do you know, within this affluent area are over fourteen thousand families living in poverty?" As she speaks her gray eyes light up with intensity and idealism reminiscent of youth. "I guess my sense of civic duty won't allow me to ignore this. Once, I even ran for State Assembly on the Republican ticket. I lost, but the experience taught me a lot. I'm a Democrat now!"

Could she have accomplished even more? "Yes. I might have risen higher in the U.N. Along the way, I went back to school again and learned to speak and write modern Greek, in addition to the three other languages I speak. Certainly I had the credentials. I am convinced now that I could have been an ambassador to the U.N."

"What do you think stopped you?" we asked. Here was a woman who had used education, intelligence, and determination to surmount every obstacle in her path. We felt like students before her.

"I was seen as threatening, even though I tried very hard to be low-key. I know I was good at my work—whenever and wherever I was doing it. But thousands of years of a certain approach to women's roles in the world isn't easily overcome in a century. I don't think we can assume that time will eventually bring equality for women, even if you allow another thousand years. We need a different approach to women's roles in the world."

For Irene, school was a source of life. Without special education, her talents might have been lost to society. Impoverished, without a family, she nevertheless was able to develop her talents, reach a point where she could show off her skills, and make a successful life for herself. Her education not only benefited her, but also the society that provided that education.

OTHER VOICES

Irene said that she had found "a home" in the classrooms of Hunter, and many other women agreed with that sentiment. Most said they loved their high school years.

Kitty, class of '33: "I was with bright, talented, smart students and thought it was a great place to be. I didn't realize it was a big deal to get in, but I was so glad to be there."

Ingrid, one of our 1950s graduates, summed up the feelings of the majority: "The benefits were the opportunity to associate with bright and talented women; an open society, where class was not a factor; healthy competition; and a warm, positive support system. We had the best education money could buy."

Renee, class of '57: "We had the run of the school and we were the center of everyone's attention. Good grades were attributed to our minds and intellect, never to that old saw, 'A for effort' or 'She's a good worker.' We didn't want to be 'good workers,' we wanted to be brilliant."

Their most vivid memories often concerned their teachers. Regina, looking back nearly seventy-five years into the past, remembered her freshman biology teacher. "She invited me to join her small nature study group. Saturday mornings around ten o'clock until noon, ten young girls met at Inwood Park, exploring shrubs, trees, and grasses, identifying leaves and blossoms. This weekly adventure with an expert nature-lover started me on a lifelong affinity with the outdoors, and later with the wilderness. Over the years, she became one of the great intellectual influences of my life, and a deep genuine affection developed between us."

Roxanne, class of '43: "My biology teacher was a dynamic, exciting person who loved us all. She was open and flexible and obviously enjoyed her work. My French teacher gave me a party when I graduated. The Hunter years made me feel special."

Sometimes their teachers were the only independent, questioning, and ambitious women these girls knew. A 1950s graduate remembered: "My parents did not encourage me to go to college; my teachers did. My parents would have been pleased if I had graduated from high school and gotten an office job."

Irene's path to success began with her having a teacher as a role model to emulate. "She didn't say I should be a teacher. I just wanted to be like her because she was so kind to me." At first Irene walked in her teacher's footsteps, creating a life based on the blueprint laid out in front of her. However, she soon began to forge into new territory. Her teacher was that rare individual who wanted her protégé to create an authentic version of herself, not merely duplicate the life of her mentor.

Second only to teachers in the affectionate memories of the Hunter women were their friendships with classmates. In this, the Hunter girls were like young women everywhere. Young friendships are the bridge between childhood and adult love. They facilitate the awful task of letting go of parents. Many Hunter girls still retain their classmates as best friends.

Cynthia, class of '67: "I was in a special advanced class in elementary school, so all the girls in my class took the test for Hunter. Four of us made it, and another girl I had known since nursery school also got in. We became the five best friends in that class—one Asian, one black, three Jews. We maintain those friendships. We have not ever missed a birthday. One of the few weddings I've been in was a Hunter girl's wedding. We graduated with the same 186 girls we started with in seventh grade, although a few girls were added in the nineth and tenth grades. We still call them 'new girls.' "

Roxanne: "My relationships with my peers were the crux of my education. They were brilliant girls, totally lacking in inhibition in class. An extraordinarily high number of girls had real character, real intensity about life. I've never been in an environment like that since."

Several women mentioned the advantages of going to an all-girls school. Renee: "There was absolutely no emphasis on any social distractions. You didn't go to school with boys, you weren't distracted by boys. There was no emphasis on clothes. We didn't go to dances. There were no distractions from the sheer business of learning and exchanging ideas. The school was electric with ideas. People were very busy expressing their individuality and making statements and developing a political consciousness. Academic excellence was a source of pride, even though at times I was very anxious about that."

Ingrid, class of '53: "I spent the formative years of my life in an atmosphere where the idea of deferring to men or 'playing dumb' was totally unknown. I met some of the wittiest, brightest, and most beautiful girls at Hunter—and I've never met their like again."

A few pointed out the disadvantages of the all-girls system.

Roxanne: "An all-girls school puts men in another world. My

fantasy was that boys would never like me, and I felt very deficient in that."

Sharon, class of '73: "I had a poor self-image in high school. Going to a single-sex school was a mixed bag. It wasn't a great idea because I didn't know a single male until I hit college and neither did my friends. The only boys we knew were from our families."

The year Sharon graduated, the first male students, eighteen of them, were admitted to Hunter High. Boys on campus sparked considerable controversy, and some women students, graduates, and members of the faculty and administration as well worried that the female students would begin to take a secondary position. An alumna from the last all-girls grade said, "Even though they were a minority, the boys were in almost all of the leadership positions. It was sickening . . . I think the girls were more submissive than they needed to be."

Factually, a significant number of those few women in top leadership positions today went to all-women colleges, and speak positively of their experience. We agree with a 1976 Hunter graduate who said, "Going to an all-girls school fostered in us a desire to succeed and a confidence in our own abilities, capabilites, and charisma. It gave us an exhilarating sense of freedom."

Several Hunter women said that after graduation they found it difficult to adjust to the outside world. One student described her loss of intellectual stimulation. "I had to learn to gear down around other people. I learned to talk to people about their interests. It made me a nicer person, and my mother liked it. The trouble is, you begin to lose your intellectual skills if you don't use them. After Hunter, I never had another place where I was intellectually challenged."

Not all Hunter women had fond memories of school. Complaints generally centered on competition and on the elitism inherent in segregating bright women from the general student population. A 1982 graduate angrily summed up her feelings: "I abhorred the elitism involved. Don't call me a gifted woman." One of my most talented classmates sent us a note saying, "I refuse to fill out your questionnaire. Hunter High was so filled with elitism and class distinctions that I want nothing to do with your research!"

Several women mentioned that the "smart" label separated them from neighborhood friends. As a consequence, loneliness and isolation, a sense of being different from others—although not really special—were common themes. Deborah, a 1970s graduate, said that her parents worried about separating her from neighborhood friends, but decided that an advantaged education would outweigh this loss. "I never regretted their decision, but I never quite recovered from the loss of my friends and the sense of security I had felt in my neighborhood school. I became something of a loner. I often felt more bewildered than bright, but I covered it up."

COMPETITION AND CLIQUES

In many ways, the educational patterns at Hunter were remarkably similar to those seen in other schools, but both the pluses and minuses seemed heightened. For example, while opportunities to learn and excel were enhanced, so was competition—the most frequently mentioned complaint among all the Hunter graduates.

As far back as 1914, Regina described herself and her classmates as "perfect little snobs. We thought we were the best, and we were." Helene, a 1960s graduate, said: "We thought all the smart people went to Hunter and everybody else was dumb. It took me a long time to learn that a lot of smart people didn't go to Hunter. It was intellectual snobbery."

A growing chorus of criticism of the social "cliques" and competition in the school emerged in the 1960s. Cynthia remembers: "Hunter had its own brand of conformity. Not in the context of athletics or social things, but in a perverse sort of antisocial behavior and certainly in terms of academic achievement. Within groups, there was very careful watching of what everybody was doing. The competition was part of that."

Cynthia and her friends called the Hunter records and guidance office "The Big Brother Room": "Room 101 was the room where all your fears were recorded. Believe me, there was your future! You would go to the records office with your friends and look up your grade point; it would be worked out to the third decimal place, and you might worry if your friends' were one digit higher. It was a very competitive place."

While academic success fostered self-esteem and pride, competition initiated fear and anxiety. Cynthia described Hunter as both rigorous and rigid: "It both stifled and encouraged one's development. I was not a good math student, and because my math grades weren't good, I was not allowed to go into special advanced English. It sapped my confidence. I was made to feel that because I was a terrible math student I was a horrible person."

Roxanne, who said she loved the attention she received from being an outstanding student, also remembered what that recognition cost her: "I felt a lot of pressure to produce something to prove that I was really as special as everyone said." Phyllis said: "The high demands led to never being satisfied with what one does."

In addition to the anxiety produced by the competitive environment, many women also described a mysterious sense of loss. Ingrid: "I learned heightened intellectual and personal standards, had access to many fine teachers, and formed enduring friendships. Yet I still feel something, I'm not sure what, was missing."

The theme of a vague "something missing" was one we would hear randomly repeated by various women. Was this "something" a factor that might have reduced their anxiety, brought their lives into an integrated whole, and sparked their ambitions? We went back and looked at the original survey, and saw immediately what was a significant part of that "missing something."

FIVE

COUNSELING: THE 911 OF EDUCATION

*"You were expected to solve your own problems
and get on with it."*

—*ROXANNE, class of '43*

Virtually every Hunter woman—whether she loved or hated school—identified one missing aspect of her education: 98 percent said they either had no counseling or that any guidance they received was "unhelpful and perfunctory." The common thread was woven through all eight decades of the study. While completing an enriched educational program most of these women had no one at Hunter whose specific job was to prepare them for obstacles and barriers in the outside world, to encourage them to pursue nontraditional roles, to inspire them to leadership. Without specific direction from counselors, they chose and pursued their careers dependent solely upon friends and family for advice.

Counselors can fill two important roles for young females. First, they can address personal and emotional problems that may be troubling a girl or holding her back in her studies. Second, counselors provide a bridge to the outside world by helping her set goals that will develop her special talents. Most Hunter girls received neither benefit.

Eileen summed up her education in the 1970s this way: "Going to Hunter was one of the best experiences of my life, but I realize now how sheltered an existence it was. We were educated in a totally different kind of world than the one outside the walls of Hunter. The real world is much harsher, much colder, and much more unforgiving."

Before the 1960s, most of the Hunter women agreed with Natalie, a 1927 graduate: "What would we have done with counseling? We knew what we were supposed to do. Go to Hunter College, become schoolteachers, and get married. We did it."

If a girl was having emotional problems, if she felt out of place and lonely, it never occurred to her to talk it over with anyone at the school. "In 1943," says Roxanne, "we weren't psychologically minded. You were expected to solve your own problems and get on with it." Similarly, if girls had difficulties coping with the competition, as many of the younger women said they did, counseling wasn't there to help alleviate the strain.

With graduates from the late 1950s, Hunter women began to express some anger over the lack of counseling. Sylvia, a graduate of the late 1950s: "With all the brains at the school, everyone could have gotten scholarships to any college in the country. But the counselors were too busy shunting everyone into becoming a teacher! Go to Hunter College was the big answer."

Ingrid, class of '53, blames her education for her fear of taking risks. "Why didn't those marvelous teachers at Hunter ever speak of our options? Why were there no seminars, no workshops, no college nights for us? How could they nurture only the intellect and ignore our emotional makeup? Did they think being smart meant we would know how to take risks? What they did not teach me at Hunter was courage."

Frieda, class of '57: "I ranked second in my graduating class. Good grades became a burden, a terrible thing to live up to. I wish someone had said, 'You don't have to be perfect all the time.' I always stayed within safe territory where I knew I could succeed. I regret I didn't even consider any other career than teaching. I regret that I didn't study science and go into medical research."

Both Ingrid and Frieda were afraid to reach into unknown territory, and both believe that with adequate counseling they could have been taught how to take risks.

Sharon, however, believes that even if counseling had been offered in the 1970s, most students wouldn't have used it: "In a place like Hunter, there was no anonymity at all. I think people would not have trusted the counselor to keep their confidentiality. There was so much competitiveness among the students, you didn't dare let anyone know you had a problem; they might learn you weren't all you were cracked up to be. Weakness could be used against you."

Instead of asking for help, these girls often did their best to hide their insecurities. Of course, this makes the counselor's role more difficult, but not impossible. Adolescents in need are seldom difficult to spot.

When Leslie, a 1969 graduate, felt overwhelmed by the pressure of constant, strenuous high performance, she sought therapy outside of school. "I knew I needed help, even though my mother was against it. I was losing weight, couldn't sleep, was bingeing and throwing up—I still do. I had a friend who was seeing a psychotherapist and thought I'd better go, too. It got me through high school, but I just went crazy afterwards. I'm still trying to get my life together."

Women of Irene's generation rarely had the problems with eating that Leslie describes. One of the alarming outcomes of the multiple pressures on women in the past twenty years has been the rise in eating disorders and food addictions, particularly among teenagers. Only 11 percent of the women in our study said they had a substance-abuse problem, but half of these said that the substance that caused problems for them was food. Eating disorders often begin with the determination of a young woman to exert control over *some* aspect of her life. In simple terms, she is saying "I will eat what I want or not eat or throw up, and you can't stop me." Even at the risk of harming herself, a woman may desperately seek to assert her own control.

Leslie made a surprising connection between eating disorders and fear. When asked "What is your greatest fear?" she answered: "Food. No, that's not it. I think it's fear of failing. Maybe it's even deeper than that. I think it's not living up to my potential."

Several women said they developed an alcohol dependency. The statistic rose over the decades until, in the 1980s, 33 percent believed they had a problem with alcohol. Toni, a 1986 graduate, said that drinking, along with drug use, was a routine part of her high school social life. "I got put on probation a couple of times at school, for getting drunk at a school dance and once for coming to school drunk, but so did lots of others."

For "good girls," the universally reported rise in addictions, from smoking to food to alcohol and drugs, mirrors the rising pressures of a society that fosters high expectations for women without addressing the realities that most women face.

During a critical life stage, when skilled professional guidance can literally save lives, most Hunter women were left to cope on their own with psychological and emotional problems. Irene, back in the 1920s, simply hung on for dear life and made it through on pluck and encouragement from her teachers. In the 1980s, Toni, like Leslie, sought counseling outside of school.

A skilled counselor might have been an enormous help to all three women. Counselors and teachers trained to observe the signs of depression and anxiety in young people (changes in weight, inability to concentrate, poor grades, alcohol- and drug-abuse) can intervene in time to stop the descent and help clear a path of recovery.

COLLEGE AND CAREER GUIDANCE

Hunter girls did not fare much better when it came to career counseling. One of the most important choice points for young women in this stage is the selection of college and major. Over 90 percent of the Hunter High graduates went on to Hunter College.

Throughout most of this century Hunter College and City College were considered the premier free colleges in the United States. Their standards were extremely high and entrance requirements were stringent. The complaints we heard from the Hunter women concerned not the quality of their college education, but their lack of choice. Irene remembered, "Everyone went on to Hunter College because it was expected and it was free."

Patricia, a 1973 graduate, said, "Hunter did nothing in terms of career guideance. We were all supposed to become teachers and now we're all going to be lawyers. What about those of us who didn't want to? We were given the routine feminine routes to follow. Period."

Helene says she was eleven years old before she ever heard the word "college." "When I was accepted at Hunter they had an orientation for parents and kids. I remember the principal saying, 'This is an academic preparatory school. There are no commercial courses here. One of the givens is that your child will be prepared to go to college. If your intention is not to send your child to college, don't send her here.'

"I turned to my mother and asked, 'Am I going to college?' She said, 'I guess so.'

"No one in our family had ever gone to college. When the time came for me to go, we didn't have the money. I didn't know I could get a scholarship, that there were loan programs, that there would be any other colleges besides Hunter that would be willing to take me. That guidance department was a disaster."

Those who were channeled into Hunter College later felt they had missed opportunities to explore different careers. In discussing her choices in this stage of life, a 1937 graduate said: "If someone could have told me this major could lead to this career, or this course might be interesting for these reasons. . . . As it was, I became a teacher for lack of any other choice." Frustration is heard in the voice of a 1950s graduate who remembers, "I wanted to be a chemical engineer and was told I'd starve in the streets, so I went into teaching." Nancy, another 1950s graduate, said, "I went to my high school reunion and found that we had mostly all attended city colleges and gone into teaching. At Hunter, they didn't lift our hopes or encourage us to break new ground. There were so many other things we could have tried."

Twenty years later, Hunter graduates, like young people everywhere, were usually confused and uncertain about which major to select. Cindy, class of '73: "I went to the guidance office for advice and was advised to take a year off and drive a taxi. My parents went wild. So I majored in education."

Always there were a few who challenged traditional expectations and chose unconventional paths. They gave little credit to their counselors. Carolyn, another 1950s graduate: "The lady sure wasn't out to expand my horizons! She acted as if I couldn't cope with the academics at a decent college. I didn't have the heart to mention that I wanted to go to medical school." Even without support from her counselor, Carolyn became a doctor.

Sharon, who drove a relentlessly straight line to a law degree, was skeptical that guidance counseling could have made a difference to her: "I don't think I would have used it. There was this feeling that you should be in control enough to know what you wanted."

Once on the college campus, things did not improve. Lauren, class of '76, who went to an all-female college on the East Coast, had an experience typical of most of the Hunter women. "I had no idea of what kind of career I wanted when I graduated. They gave us a good party when we graduated. The business majors got to meet with the ten companies that go to every college campus in the country, such as IBM and 3M. But the rest of us—the anthropology and sociology majors, the music majors, the English majors—nobody got anything beyond 'Here's your report card.' When graduation came, there was nothing to prepare us for anything that was going to happen beyond the day we wore the robes."

High school and college counselors are only one link in a complex chain that leads young women into the larger world. Parents are another. Many women told us how their parents, particularly their mothers, helped and encouraged them to go on to college. One of our oldest women, a 1911 graduate, says, "My mother had wanted to go to college, but never finished high school. Since that desire was never fulfilled, my mother believed I should be permitted to go, to do anything her son could do. There was no sex discrimination in our household! Off I went."

Several women from the earlier decades described the hope their immigrant parents held for their children. A 1929 graduate tells us, "My parents believed education was the road to the future—money, success, security. They wanted all of us to have the best in terms of education." These were the children of hopeful new Americans at the beginning of the century. But for daughters, the striving for a better life often ended with a diploma. Upon high school and college graduation, most Hunter women across the decades said their parents had only vague expectations for their future.

A 1950s graduate says, "My parents wanted me to be able to support myself without resorting to hard physical labor, but that was the most guidance I received." Another from the same decade summed up the prevailing parental attitude: "My parents expected me to finish college, but no one cared whether I became an engineer, teacher, doctor, or whatever. Mom was a schoolteacher, so that's what I did."

Several Hunter women told us that their parents' vague goals for them contrasted sharply with those set for their brothers. A graduate from 1928 said: "I was accepted at Cornell, but didn't go because my father said he didn't have the money. However, he shelled out more than we could afford toward my brother's education. At that time, we didn't think of it as discrimination."

Fifty years later, Gina, a 1979 grad, told us about her two brothers. "From the time they were little, they planned to be lawyers and that's what they did. But I didn't have any interests that I could come up with. I figured when I started college that something would come to me."

When Gina graduated, she still had no clear idea about what she wanted to do. She earned a teaching certificate, but realized she had little commitment to education. "Maybe because my brothers seemed to know their course so early I considered myself a throwaway, a floater. I thought my scores and grades were just a fluke. It wasn't until years later I realized that I had as much going for me—maybe even more—than my brothers. It took me so damn long to believe that I was smart and to do something with my life. I got some help, some therapy, and pursued and advanced degree in science. I'm a professor at a university and feel I've found my calling. But I never even heard the call u?

CHANGE FOR THE FUT

Although the Hunter wome. tellectual rigor in high school, the groomed for leadership. From earliest ch. tradictory and diminishing messages that shap society. Research shows that even before they go know the sexual behavior patterns expected of then. school and kindergarten, children begin to internalize the sex roles. Their behavior is reinforced by parents and teache. consistently reward little girls who are modest, obedient to author, and sensitive to the needs of others.

For the Hunter women, the people in the best position to encourage their Active Engagement—school counselors and teachers—most often had set them on traditional paths. In this regard, Hunter is no different from most schools. If independent choice had not happened here, in this rarified atmosphere, we can surmise that it has not happened in most high schools across the country.

Nor had the Hunter women been able to use friendships in the same way that men do. Helene: "Women have such a remarkable capacity for friendship, but somehow it doesn't translate. Think of all the successful men who do business with their college friends. It boggles the mind." The Hunter women carried their friendships into adult life, but relied on them primarily for emotional support.

If a woman's gift for friendship could be applied to the professional and business world—teamwork based on trust, vulnerability, loyalty—women would be able to help each other through the obstacles that remain at the top.

Role models, too, were lacking. The most frequently cited role models were teachers, who, although they held their pupils to a high standard of academic achievement, emphasized traditional feminine pursuits. Teachers also imparted a strong sense of social obligation and service to others. Mabel, a 1929 graduate: "Our teachers emphasized that we had an obligation to use our intellect to serve and to contribute. Our training at Hunter discouraged thinking of ourselves as special."

Mabel saw this as a positive trait and, indeed, using one's potential for benefit of the greater good is a tradition worth emulating. However, modesty and dedication to others dovetails almost too neatly into learning to deny one's intelligence. After surviving a strenuous selection process and receiving an enriched education, Hunter women, according to Mabel, had been encouraged *not* to think of themselves as "special."

What teachers neglected to do in many instances was to show their young female students how to serve society and still fulfill their own visions. Leadership itself may not be a woman's goal in life, but every woman should have the opportunity to choose independently her own course. If leadership is her goal, she needs to be groomed for it.

To overcome negative conditioning, girls need specific training to show them how to pursue the nontraditional and make their own choices independent of the expectations of their times. Even in grade school teachers can help girls develop pride in accomplishments, pleasure in physical prowess, and independent judgment—leadership traits often seen as masculine. Teachers can show that these traits are human—neither masculine nor feminine.

Counselors in the secondary schools can reinforce the work that teachers have begun. The influence of counselors is critical at this age because adolescence requires girls to separate from their parents and establish their own identities. In order to do this, they need "transitional figures," adult women who will demonstrate and promote leadership skills in their students.

Female role models can be held up whose lives illustrate a variety of satisfying and nontraditional lifestyles. Creative, nontraditional counselors themselves can serve as role models. Girls can be asked to imagine their lives in the future: What do they see for themselves? What barriers do they imagine they would face in reaching their goals? What are the strategies and who are the helpers they might call upon to surmount those barriers?

Sports and athletics, in which Hunter was lacking until recently, are another way women learn both teamwork and leadership. Almost all the women in Fortune 500's top executives, although minuscule in number compared to men, said that as youngsters they were active in team sports.

Lauren, class of '76: "Recently I received a letter from the alumni association of my college soliciting money for a sports arena to attract male students. When I was there it was still a girls' school and there were no sports. Athletics were not considered important for women. They still aren't. The new sports compound is for the boys."

Young girls need teachers and counselors working along with parents who encourage them to explore and experiment, to develop visions and dreams about futures that are foreign to their culture and times. They need to imagine themselves as leaders and heroes, healers and teachers, producers and presidents. To prepare themselves for these roles, they need to hear the voices of teachers, counselors, role models, and friends cheering them on, a chorus of encourgement to their achievements.

SIX

CHOOSING WORK

I just tripped over my career.

— *ROSEMARIE, class of '69*

With little counseling and limited or vague expectations from their families, how did Hunter women choose their careers? Women who graduated before the 1970s said that when it came to deciding what kind of work to do, few choices were available:

AMELIA, class of '09: "There was no real choice. If we worked, we were expected to be teachers or secretaries."

BERTHA, class of '10: "Our choices were between low-pay clerical jobs or being housewives and mothers. I stayed home with my children."

CLARA, class of '19: "I wanted something more exciting. I chose social work, which seemed a new and rewarding alternative to teaching or secretarial work."

The rationale behind women choosing jobs in these decades was that work was incidental to marriage and children. Employers did not expect women to stay on the job and made no plans for their advancement. Women who wished to work after marriage usually chose to teach school because it fit smoothly within a family framework.

Occasionally, an older woman told us she had imagined a nontraditional career, but quickly renounced it. Sylvia, a late '50s graduate: "My ambition to obtain a medical degree was never countenanced. A five-foot-one-inch female doctor? Be serious!"

The few women who chose nontraditional careers often were seen as frustrated in love and sex. They were the women who flew planes, started businesses, climbed mountains, went to Africa. They were often admired, on the one hand, and denigrated on the other.

PHYLLIS, class of '58: "I remember the career-woman movies in the forties. The underlying message was she couldn't be really happy unless she got married and settled down. In real life, I didn't see any women running companies. Maybe they were, but it certainly wasn't in my consciousness."

INGRID, class of '53: "At school, we were trained, groomed, and prepared for a world that had little place for our talents. A few of us became doctors and lawyers, judges and corporate executives. The rest of us needed someone to tell us 'Take courage in your hands, make the unconventional leaps.' No one did."

Throughout the century, the first line of influence was parents who shaped their daughters' aspirations and also their attitude toward work. Renee, class of '57, CEO of a major advertising agency: "Because my mother was an advertising woman—a pioneer in a field that was closed to women—I grew up believing that success in work was desirable and honorable for women."

ROXANNE, class of '43, received a mixed message from her parents: "When I got into Hunter my parents gave me my own room, which was a tremendous sacrifice of space of the household. They also gave me a solid oak desk, which I still have. They urged me to work for a scholarship. Yet for all the encouragement, my mother thought men should lead, and that women should follow. I never internalized a sense of being valuable in my own right, and I think that affected my career choice. I wanted to be a college professor, but my mother said I should teach elementary school."

Some studies have suggested that the combination of a working mother, supportive father, and well-educated parents provide the best family environment for influencing a successful daughter. Yet this privileged scenario, even when present for the Hunter women, produced varying results. There was no magical family tableau that guaranteed high aspirations. Most of the women before 1950 grew up in two-parent families, while fewer of the women after 1950 did so. Several depended on their single mothers for reassurance and esteem, and in a few cases their dependence was extreme.

The radicalism of the late 1960s changed the way women viewed their opportunities, and lives of the Hunter graduates reflected those changes. Many older Hunter women told us that they envy the young women of today. Clara, class of '19, said wistfully: "I think that today's women have fewer conflicts than my generation. They are aware of their options and choices. We never had any."

ESTHER, class of '14: "Women today seem to know what they want and go after it. I envy that. People I knew didn't take jobs."

In a sense, young women today stand on the shoulders of mothers, grandmothers, suffragettes, and pioneers. Susan, an astronautical physicist, class of '75: "Studies in engineering, medicine, and law were never barred to my generation of women, so I became a scientist. I ventured forth with a kind of blind confidence that I could do anything, and fortunately it has been enough to carry me through, at least so far."

The older Hunter women tended to simplify the ease with which younger women pursue their new opportunities. Many 1980s graduates in our study who assume that they will go after any job they wish, marry, and have children are often unclear about how they are supposed to do this.

TONI, class of '86: "We have enormous expectations. We're supposed to have careers, get married, have children—I don't have a clue how to do all this."

EMILY, class of '77, who has already logged in ten years in a high-paying banking job: "Does anybody else have the problem with knowing what they want to do? The point these days is to find the thing in life you feel passionately about, and pursue that as your life's work. I'm thinking, 'How on earth do I know what that is?' "

Several women agreed with Emily and said they believed they could make a choice if only they could identify a passion in life.

EMILY: "The problem is that you're always doing what's expected, living up to the image. Even hobbies—my husband has a zillion hobbies, and things that he's interested in and spends money on. My hobby is cleaning house."

Young women today obviously have greater career opportunities than their mothers ever dreamed of. In the United States, women comprise 43 percent of the overall work force. Since the early 1970s women have increased their presence in law, medicine, and business by 300 to 400 percent. And for the first time in history, women make up more than half of university students.

However, women still assume most of the responsibility for childcare and home management, and face a continuing struggle toward equal pay and promotion.

SHARON, class of '73: "It's easy to see why there aren't as many women leaders. How many women have had uninterrupted careers? How many six-figure incomes are controlled by women even now? I'm one of three female partners in my law firm out of a possible twenty-five, so things are changing—but sometimes it seems like a glacially slow process."

To some degree the same fears and worries that haunted the class of 1910, haunt the graduates of the 1970s and 1980s. Despite greater options and opportunities, younger Hunter women still make career choices in much the same way as their predecessors. We heard it many times, from many different women: career choices were made in order to live up to parental expectations or by sheer accident; sometimes they were never made at all.

We looked closely at the way three more recent graduates chose their present careers.

THE STRAIGHT ARROW

James Hillman, who for ten years served as director of studies at the C. G. Jung Institute in Zurich, has said, "We are not motivated to act by reason or by reinforcement, but by fantasy—the images and myths with which we have grown up." It is in childhood that a girl's fantasies about work begin to form, based on the images projected by her parents. When she was still in kindergarten Sharon already understood that her parents' expectations for her were very high and very specific.

"Both my parents were first-generation immigrants who had worked their way through law school, and they wanted me to follow in their footsteps. They instilled in me the hard-driving immigrant mentality that sees education as the road to achievement. For them, and for me, the law was not merely a career, it was a magnificent obsession. We believe in it the way you believe in a religion. I was proud to think I would grow up to be a lawyer.

"As a child, I wanted to go to Radcliffe. When I was a teenager, I wanted to go to Yale, because it was the hardest one to get into. I would have felt like a terrible failure if I hadn't gotten in to Yale, Princeton, or Harvard."

The enriched atmosphere at Hunter was the first step on Sharon's road to law school. She attended high school during an explosive time in history. "We spent our entire senior year in the school auditorium participating in demonstrations against the United States involvement in Cambodia. The second half of the year we talked about the role of education, and the students in running the school. Some of Hunter's funny little traditions—the Senior Sing and choosing mascots—were bypassed that year in favor of student demonstrations. In the 1970s we were on the brink of so many things. The women's movement, civil rights, the sexual revolution. I can't separate my life from these things, yet I wasn't tremendously caught up in any one of them. My parents—and my education—were the greatest motivating factors for me."

Sharon did go to Princeton, and found the atmosphere at

college thin compared to her experience at Hunter. "College was not as stimulating. It hadn't caught up with New York." She was surprised during her first semester at Harvard Law School to discover blatant biases toward women students. "We were all brought into the auditorium where the president of the university outlined his vision of educating the 'One Thousand Male Leaders of the Twenty-First Century.' Two hundred of us were women. You know we had to have had better credentials than the male students to even be in the class. Yet for the president, we didn't exist. This was 1974. I wrote angry articles to the campus paper, but it didn't change anything."

We asked Sharon if she had ever considered any other career. "Briefly, when I was in college, I questioned my plan, thinking that I might like to do something else. But my parents refocused me and I fulfilled their expectations. I've never regretted it."

After graduating from Harvard, Sharon joined a prestigious law firm in Washington, D.C. "I never considered any other kind of practice. It had to be the biggest, most important firm, where I could make an impact and get recognition. My goal was to make partner in seven years. I made it in six. I was the first female partner in my firm. Many more women are lawyers today, but becoming a partner is much harder. I knocked myself out."

How authentic was Sharon's choice? She prepared early for her career and followed through on her goals without interruption, which makes her unusual among those Hunter women who also had forged careers. However, like most women over the century, she still made her choices based on the specific expectations of her parents. She was a good girl of the 1970s—her single-minded determination led to contemporary rewards, but did not include any period of exploration. Sharon is successful and achieving, but did her career choice spring from a clear sense of self?

"Yes, I think it did. I never felt I needed to be anything but what I am. I give my parents a lot of credit. I guess you could say they imposed their choices on me, but I was a ready recipient. I think if I had said I wanted to do something else, they would have supported me. As it was, what they wanted, I wanted for myself. This is who I am."

Sharon is unique in several ways, most notably in that her goals were set early and she progressed in work without interruption—no periods of confusion, no time off to meet needs of others, no self-doubt.

She denigrates her younger sister's lifestyle. "Somehow my sister got a different message. She has a different attitude toward work and life than I do. She has the marriage, the child. She works in television, but her husband's income is far greater than hers, and he really supports the family.

"To me the critical issue is whether women earn the same pay as men. In a law firm, the issues are not about titles—it's about economics. You are treated the same way as your peers only if you earn as much. Money commands respect. If you're not earning as much as the men in your workplace you're not getting the same level of respect or opportunity."

Sharon's method of choosing a career is remarkably similar to the method used by women of earlier decades who said "We knew what was expected, and we did it." The big difference is that in Sharon's decade, the expectation had changed and so had the opportunities. In almost direct contrast to Sharon's self-assured approach is Joyce's story.

THE SLEEPING PRINCESS

When faced with career options that neither their mothers nor grandmothers ever enjoyed, many young women said they felt confused and even paralyzed. Despite social changes, many did not see themselves as capable of controlling and directing their futures.

Joyce, class of '82, was one of the first recipients of Hunter's outreach to minority children. Unlike Sharon, who had two proactive parents, Joyce lived alone with her mother and depended heavily upon her for reassurance and support.

"I grew up on 112th Street in Harlem, but I went to school on the East Side. Most of my friends in school were rich and white. As a middle-class black child I spent summers at their homes in the Hamptons and winters visiting in their Park Avenue apartments."

We asked if she was uncomfortable in those settings. "We never talked about race. We pretended to believe that the same future and the same opportunities awaited us all. I say 'pretended'—it wasn't conscious pretense. We just didn't deal with it. I was a pretty little girl and well behaved, and I tried to fit in wherever I was invited. I got by.

"My mother did everything for me when I was growing up. All my choices were made by talking to my mom first. I tend to shy away from risks, although there have been times I would try certain things with a failure factor as long as my mother said it was all right. All she asked was that I study and get top grades in school, which I always did. The very top. I knew I was different from other kids where we lived. I had to be the best. I couldn't ever fail."

Joyce inherited her mother's pride in achievement, along with a subliminal fear that she might not live up to high parental standards. Her mother was a middle manager at Con Edison, and Joyce had vague dreams of making a career in "business." Both mother and daughter believed that Joyce's academic achievements would mainstream into similar success in the outside job market.

Joyce attended Barnard College. "It was like repeating my last three years at Hunter." After graduating from college, Joyce joined Bloomingdale's management training program. Two years later she switched to a "dream job" in a large advertising agency, where she advanced rapidly. "I got wonderful praise and I deserved it. After seven months I received a service award for 'Best Employee.' I was the youngest person ever to get it. I loved the recognition. I was a winner, just as I had been in school. And then, wham, I lost it. All the newer people were let go. My supervisor said all the right things, but I still had to walk out the door. I was devastated. I had never failed before. I felt so degraded. I went to the unemployment office, tears streaming down my face."

Joyce tried to find the resources to repair this injury to her self-esteem, but nothing in her past had prepared her to deal with failure. Her success in school had led her to believe that if she performed brilliantly she would always be rewarded. She did not know how to grapple with a world that often hands out defeat to even the best of the best.

"I thought bad girls wound up pregnant and on dope. And good girls like me, who turned in a brilliant performance, rose steadily to the top. That's not how it works. You can do it all right and still get kicked in the teeth. No one had ever told me that."

Joyce's problems were compounded when her mother retired and moved to Atlanta. "My whole development was based on an underlying kindred bonding with my mother. When I was a child I used to imagine I could die if my mother didn't come home. Now, the ground's shaking and I'm at the bottom of the pole—and no Mom. I fall into deep depressions, wondering what my life is all about."

Joyce is aware that her dependence on her mother has delayed her own growth. Joyce also admits that as a black child and woman, she had few role models, other than her mother. Joyce had grown up so praised and guided by her mother and her teachers that she now expects someone else to recognize her talents and direct her future. "I see now that I've never had to make a choice in my life."

After three months of searching, Joyce found a new job with IBM in their sales department. "I went to a big job fair being held at the Hilton. I went right to the IBM table and really wowed them with my blah blah. My mother always told me I could sell dirt to a farmer. They invited me to come in for an interview; I interviewed with five executives and the last one offered me a job in sales. I had to latch on to whatever rope I could, so I took it."

Joyce took the sales job out of desperation, and finds it disappointing and unrewarding. Forced to compete and try hard for a job with little challenge or excitement, a job she needs to pay the bills, she is for the first time facing up to a harsh reality: "When I think about the future I realize I have no goals. My boyfriend is a graphics designer. He was born with this talent and he went to a very artsy college and studied design. He has a passion for what he does. I don't have a goal like that to pursue."

Her inability to take control of her future has Joyce on an emotional roller coaster, trundling between depression and panic. "I think I might like to be a teacher, because I love children and I would be terrific. But teachers don't make any money. Would this be a good choice? Here I am, selling a copier to some jerk. It drives me crazy. No one ever told me I would have to decide these things for myself. I guess I thought they would just continue to give me tests and I would continue to do well."

Joyce faces a critical choice point: stay with IBM or try to find work that is more rewarding. For the first time she is coming to terms with the fact that as a black woman her career options might be limited. The idea that equal opportunity is said to exist for everyone, despite race or gender, confuses a lot of women. While Joyce is told she is smart enough to do anything she wants with her life, she is still largely unaware that there are obstacles in the workplace. She blames herself for her confusion and wonders what's wrong with her.

The career a woman chooses depends on how she perceives her choices. Opportunities in every decade are always limited by family expectations, economic necessities, social patterns, and legal regulations. Some firms still have corporate policies that say women can work only below particular levels and in a limited range of tasks. The U.S. military holds women back from higher ranks by excluding them from combat duty, although jet fighter pilots are a recent exception. Professional baseball says women don't have what it takes to be umpires or work in managerial or front-office positions. Subtle or unspoken discrimination is tougher for women of color. Limited opportunities mean diminished motivation.

It takes unique courage to be the first woman in an all-male field, and/or the first black in an all-white field. Women need special preparation and encouragement—from parents, teachers, and counselors—to withstand the criticism and rejection that inevitably accompanies such acts. In Joyce's case, no one has even told her that the road ahead might be rough.

Joyce is having trouble gaining a direction in her life because she doesn't have a clear picture of what she's up against, because her goals are unclear, and because she has never been encouraged to take risks. The irony is that Joyce, apparently with more options open to her than her older Hunter classmates, still wants to teach school. Yet she has also been swayed by the values of the times— ambition, advancement, money, and status. However, she recognizes within herself another set of values taught by her family and school—helping others, finding meaning in work, giving to children the time and attention which she was given. The difference between Joyce and the Hunter grads of earlier decades who were channeled into teaching is that Joyce is in a position to make a true choice for herself based on her own personal values.

THE LUCKY KLUTZ

While work attitudes and career aspirations begin in childhood, awareness of one's real possibilities are more concretely grasped during the teenage years. Schools repeat and reinterpret the images and myths of childhood, usually incorporating the biases of society into the child's vision.

In many ways, Hunter, by setting standards based on intellectual achievement, was an exception to the usual high school environment. Not every Hunter woman enjoyed the academic atmosphere, though.

ROSEMARIE, class of '69: "As a small child I had already learned that academic success wasn't desirable. I lived with my mother in Brooklyn and attended public elementary school. I was a perfect example of the shy, sensitive egghead, and the other kids constantly made fun of me."

Rosemarie's working mother, herself isolated, was unable to help her daughter fit in. "My mother knew what was going on, but she didn't know how to deal with it. She was a secretary and didn't have the time, or perhaps the educational background, to understand how to help me.

"I think my mother's lack of education affected how she reared me. She wasn't aware of a lot of options for me or for herself. She was a smart person who just never had much opportunity to develop herself. How could she help me?"

The bias underlying this question, that mothers contribute little to their daughters' vocations, is common. Yet Rosemarie admits that her mother did influence her sense of independence. "Looking back on it now, the fact that my mother supported both of us, without help, profoundly colored my life. I grew up thinking it was normal for a woman to bring home the bacon. On the downside, I'm very uncomfortable with the idea of marriage and almost pathological about being financially independent. I'm uneasy in any relationship where the man pays for my share. I think the person with the money is in charge. If that's the case, I want that person to be me."

Her elementary school education taught Rosemarie to hide her gifts and shy away from other students. "When I placed first in the Hunter entrance exams, I was terrified the other students would find out and their teasing would be worse than ever."

The Hunter test was Rosemarie's ticket out of Brooklyn and away from schoolmates who taunted her. However, the damage had been done. Bespectacled and chubby, Rosemarie remained wary of her new, more glamorous classmates in Manhattan. "I missed a lot of the exciting stuff that was going on at Hunter because I was trying to hide in the background. I was unaware of the competition and the challenge. High school was just something else I had to get through.

"I had a bad time as a teenager. My mother loved me, but she had no idea of what was going on in my head. We lived in a cramped two-room apartment, sort of glued together, two people related by blood, with nothing in common. My most vivid memory was feeling trapped and smothered. All I looked forward to was getting out."

Rosemarie had little to fall back on in terms of other family members. But like a lot of smart youngsters who learn to survive, Rosemarie attracted adults who could provide the emotional support she needed. "I baby-sat for a couple in the neighhborhood who became surrogate parents to me. The mother was a graduate of Sarah Lawrence. She was sympathetic, literate, and just opened a whole new world for me. I was all shriveled up inside; she just unfolded me. She and her husband encouraged me to go to college. With them I felt an element of rationality, a rapport, that I couldn't seem to find with my own mother. In a lot of ways, my future hinged on them."

Looking back on it now, Rosemarie sees the choices she made in her late teens as a series of nondecisions. "I was always running away, rather than choosing something to go toward. I accepted a scholarship to Sarah Lawrence because it would get me out of the house. But a socially rich campus was an uncomfortable place for a girl like me. My mother and I lived on the edge of poverty. I had never learned how to make friends and things didn't change much in college. I remained a misfit all the way through.

"I was never aware of needing to choose a career. I never even thought about it. After college, I moved down to Atlanta because my boyfriend got a job there. I found a job in a bank by accident when someone at a party told me about an opening.

"I went on to investment management because that's what was happening. When I started, it felt like a good way to go. Everybody had cars and condos, vacation houses and designer everything. I guess you could say money was fashionable."

In the beginning of the high-flying 1980s, Rosemarie earned an M.B.A. at Wharton and soared on up in the financial industry. She is now senior investment analyst for one of the largest brokerage houses in Wall Street. There is no trace of the clumsy adolescent in the erect, confident woman sitting across from us. She is businesslike, somewhat hurried during the interview.

"A lot of people find me intimidating," she says. When I seemed surprised, she counters, "I'm trying to hide it. I realize I put people off, and I'm deliberately trying to tone down my style."

Rosemarie sees her life as a series of fortunate stumbles, rather than conscious choices. She is the lucky klutz, someone who is smart enough to take advantage of opportunities that come her way. "I tripped over my career. I have a sense of my own history as being a product of falling into things. I think it's my nature." Her language is similar to many women we interviewed who said that they just happened upon a lucky break or "bumped into" jobs without acknowledging their own intentions in seeking those opportunities.

Men also stumble into career opportunities. However, the true leaders—both male and female—quickly regain their footing, size up their surroundings, put their abilities to work, and move ahead. They risk taking the necessary steps that allow them to emerge triumphant and achieve.

Even though Rosemarie believes she found her life's work by accident, she still had to achieve in school, steer her life in a given direction, and eventually find work which would challenge her. She views her early period of exploration as "immaturity." "Some people just aren't ready to be intrigued yet in their twenties. They need more time."

This fits with the life-cycle theory that views the twenties as a period of flux. It also fits with something we learned about smart women: the tendency to hold back, to deny that they have a right to set high goals and to achieve them. Few women in our study, in any decade, took full responsibility for choosing their own work and pursuing it to its ultimate end.

On reflection, Rosemarie admits that perhaps she was making choices for herself, without realizing it. "Perhaps I set things up so that the choices become the obvious ones. I chose to go to Sarah Lawrence; to leave my boyfriend; to get my M.B.A. These were choices, but they were never accompaniend by a lot of major soul-searching or flagellation. They just seemed like the right thing to do at the time, and they turned out all right."

Many Hunter women told a similar story. For the most part, like Rosemarie, they said their accidental choices turned out well for them, although a few admitted regrets:

LILLIAN, class of '50: "Being a professor of languages and literature may well be what I'm best suited for, but I wish I had consciously chosen it, rather than just falling into it."

LOIS, class of '59: "At a pivotal time in my life I wanted to move to Los Angeles to pursue a film writing career, but I was in love with a New Yorker. I thought if I left I'd lose him. Ultimately, I was more interested in helping my boyfriend find *himself* than I was in pursuing my own goals. We got married. I write technical books now for the computer industry. If I had it to do again? I would have gone to California."

RENEE, class of '67: "I regret that I didn't have more of a career focus early on. I regret that I allowed myself to be vague and sort of go with the flow. I regret that I didn't have more self-determination, because although it ended up wonderfully, it was painful. I think if I had been more in control of my own destiny at an earlier age, with more direction and focus, I might have been spared some of that pain I experienced getting to where I am now.

"I don't know to this day what got in the way of my doing this. To some extent, I think I was rebelling against my mother. I thought she had too much direction. Maybe it was the times. The sixties were so anti-Establishment. We thought we didn't have to worry about the future or what we would do with our lives. We lived for the moment. My friends and I were all quite privileged with our college educations. I thought I'd be an artist type and that my life would be easy and freewheeling. It didn't turn out that way. Finally, I realized that you can't live your whole life by trial and error, that you need to have a goal."

Rosemarie says that she has no such regrets. "I'm a lot happier in the last fifteen or twenty years, and most of that is due to my financial and professional success. Yes, occasionally I wonder if I should be doing some other kind of work. When I first came here, I assumed that it would be temporary, that I would go off and do some other work in keeping with my populist roots. I would like to be free to do that, but I've become used to the life-style and the money. It would be difficult for me to do work that meant a drastic cut in pay. Partly because I'm used to it and, partly, there were just certain things drummed into me at an early age. Avoid being poor. It's hard to kick."

Rosemarie's choice of a career in the financial industry is an interesting one. She's not the first person from an economically deprived background to seek wealth and financial security. But when Rosemarie made the move, she closed the door on her past.

"I don't think about the past. I realize there are a lot of things about the way in which I grew up that I probably have never dealt with. I wonder, do you really have to deal with the past? I think you can get beyond it and move on."

Important patterns of choice emerged from these stories. Throughout the century women have chosen careers largely by accident or by social or familial pressure.

Sharon, guided by her parents, knew even as a small child that she wanted to study law. She had a clear sense of her vocational future, set her goal, and found the means to accomplish it. There was little deliberation or ambivalence about her decision. Her choice was not preceded by a period of exploration that usually characterizes effective decision-making. One questions whether in midlife Sharon will have a crisis of meaning, where she begins to wonder if she has missed something.

Joyce, the "sleeping princess," had been so sheltered that when she failed in her first tentative steps into the business world, she ran back to the tower, waiting to be rescued. Joyce still sees her future as trial and error, until magically someone gives her the right opportunity and she finds her "niche."

Joyce is struggling to halt the casual drift that threatens to overtake her life. Although she seems to be floundering, she is in a good position to become actively engaged. She has met with rejection, felt the pain of failure, and is trying to recover by using the many tools of her growing years to promote herself. She recognizes the problem that faces her: "I have to decide what I want and go after it, instead of expecting someone else to recognize my abilities and provide the right slot."

Rosemarie, the daughter of a divorced mother who struggled as a secretary to support her, didn't know what she wanted to do with her life until she "tripped" over an opportunity and pursued it. She is typical of many Hunter women who could not admit that they planned and strived for a successful career. The appeal of stumbling into a career is that the individual can't be blamed if things don't turn out well. The danger is the likelihood that by "going with the flow," she will miss her true calling.

Not Sharon, Rosemarie, nor Joyce aspired to top leadership. For the present, their dreams seem to "top out" in the middle kingdom. Missing are certain key elements critical in preparing for leadership.

Women aspiring to leadership have to be willing to tolerate a period of exploration and uncertainty before identifying a life's passion. This is an essential part of making a choice. Exploration, although sometimes uncomfortable, is quite distinct from a stagnant period of drift that fogs the mind and prevents Active Engagement.

Women also have to be willing to take chances and be able to recover quickly if they fail. Ultimately, before anyone can lead and have others follow, she must be willing to admit that she aspires to leadership. Women need to declare their intentions and to imagine themselves living out life at the top. The crux for each of us is that we make a conscious choice, risking both the consequences and possibilities of that choice.

SEVEN

WORKING: STRUGGLE FOR THE TOP

The higher up you go, the stronger the isolation gets.

—*EILEEN, class of '72*

THE WAY THINGS WERE

When it came to their views on opportunities for women in the workplace, there was no clear pattern among the Hunter women. Some said, "No problem"; others raged at inequalities they encountered. The discrepancy in their perceptions stemmed partly from a generation gap. The older women tended to envy the opportunities younger women have today and were often critical of their desire to work their way up. For their part, the younger women often failed to appreciate the hard road traveled by their recent predecessors in the workplace, and some were amazed to hear stories of discrimination practiced against women just a few brief decades ago.

When her father died in 1936, Kitty left Hunter College at the end of her junior year to help support her mother. "My brothers offered to help me stay in school, but I couldn't see that. I quit. I don't know why I thought this was my role, but I did."

At the height of the Depression, Kitty went job-hunting. "Everyone was out of work. I remember going on one job interview wearing my Phi Beta Kappa key—the man who admired the key was admiring the neckline of the dress more. I was lucky—because I had been a math major I got a job in the accounting department of a department store chain. The starting salary was sixteen dollars a week, big money in those days.

"My job was mostly filing. I opened the mail and they taught me office routines. I was grateful to have a place to go. When the war came, the head of the accounting department quit to have a baby to keep her husband from the draft. Since she expected to come back, I got a temporary promotion into her job, at my same salary. Since I was now an executive, they also stopped paying me for overtime. I guess you could say they got more bang for their bucks.

"I remember the boss's wife telling me, 'You're a fool not to demand more.' Well, this was just the way things were. I had a good job and I bought the line they gave me. It was a nice place to work and I felt important there.

"One time the company was looking for a new assistant treasurer. Management spent all afternoon in the president's office trying to decide who would get the job. This story was later told to me by my boss. They mentioned a man who was head of one department and said he couldn't get along with people; they mentioned a man from another department and said he had too many outside interests. At the end of the day, they hadn't chosen anyone. My boss said that all afternoon they kept saying, 'If only Miss S— were a man!' I used to think that was a flattering story!

"During the war, for the first time women became managers. As the war ended, we wined and dined the men as they came home. The men stepped back into their jobs as store managers and division heads. I felt that was right, that they were entitled. I was like Rosie the Riveter, keeping the company going until the men came back.

"In my whole working life, I never earned as much as my male counterparts. My top salary at McClellan's was eighty-five dollars a week."

GLADYS, class of '27: "We didn't consider it discrimination in those days. When your boss said your male counterpart would earn more than you because he had a family, it seemed rational."

ANNA, class of '29: "I was always paid one-half of the salary of men on the job. As head of a small section of a social work agency, I did casework with the elderly. I stayed for thirty years. I chose not to move up because I liked my job, and I didn't feel that ambitious."

Roxanne went job-hunting for the first time in 1945: "I applied to teach French literature at the college level and was told that I didn't 'need' the job as much as a male who would head a household."

MATTIE, class of '57: "A woman was seen as dabbling at work, until she met her husband, so the pay scale was different. They believed she would be subsidized by her husband, or supported by her parents, or live off a trust fund. Or, she simply didn't need much money."

In the 1960s, as more and more people began to question the status quo, poorer, weaker segments of society started to demand equal rights, most notably blacks in the civil rights movement and women in the beginning of the women's movement. At its peak in the 1970s, the women's movement increased expectations for fuller participation for women in all levels of society, most notably the work arena. Yet, despite changes, in many ways the words remain the same:

Lauren, class of '76, describes her male counterpart on the job today: "Mike and I are exactly equal in responsibility and potential. We have the same title, the same kind of office, the same authority within the company. The only difference is that he makes thirty thousand dollars more a year than I do, and works half the number of hours."

STRUGGLE FOR THE TOP: PLAYING POLITICS

MICHELLE, class of '74: "My education did not prepare me for the political games necessary in the corporate environment. I didn't want to take on the worst characteristics found in a paternalistic and sexist atmosphere to survive. I didn't want to lose the feminine qualities I came in with. I saw this as a real dilemma and I still do."

GRACE, class of '68: "Either way, you're going to get criticized. Women who are a little tough and aggressive, there's always some nasty dig about not being feminine. On the other hand, when a woman executive tries to bridge that gap, wears very feminine dresses, she gets put down for that, too. Where do power and aggressiveness and ambition fit in with the stereotype of being feminine and sexy and cajoling and flirtatious? It's very hard. Women who are as aggressive as men are called bitches."

LAUREN, who does new business for a large interior design firm: "Do you know how they position me at work? They say I'm 'very results-oriented, very organized, no-nonsense, productive.' The they say, 'In a nutshell—she's a bitch on wheels.' I'm thinking, 'How would they describe a man with the same characteristics?' "

SANDRA, class of '70, research biologist: "I've seen two kinds of women make it to the top. The chairman of my department is a woman, and she has tunnel vision. The lab is her life. She doesn't take care of herself. She's known as a total eccentric, but she's world-famous for her work, so no one can argue with her success.

"The other woman I had as a boss was just the opposite. She flirted with everybody nonstop. She was more of a politician. She doesn't do brilliant work, nobody reads her papers—but she's phenomenally successful. She's very good-looking and she knew how to parlay it. In a way she behaved like a man, in the political sense, buttering people up, but with an utterly feminine look."

•

Hunter women from all decades said they enjoyed hands-on work, and resisted self-promotion and office politics. "Love the work, hate the politics" was almost universal language among them. Eileen, a 1972 graduate, who at age thirty-six has climbed the upper rungs of middle management in one of the nation's largest food distribution companies, told us that to get ahead she forced herself to become more political.

EILEEN: "Women will work fourteen, eighteen hours a day— to get the best product, the business plan, the best whatever. That 'best job' aspect undeniably has to be there. In my opinion, professionally speaking, women all along the line have to be twice as good in the job as men. That's a simple fact. Men can get away with mediocrity, women can't."

ISOLATED AT THE TOP

Next to politics and self-promotion, Hunter women cited isolation as the most common problem they faced in working up to top leadership. Eileen: "My entire career, I have always been one of one or two females on the staff. No doubt about it, being female means the men are less willing to take you into their confidence and more likely to shut you out of decision-making. The higher up you go, the stronger the isolation gets."

Several women told us that they didn't feel they could rely on women bosses to give them a leg up. "Women can be worse than men when it comes to power trips," said Carolyn, class of '70, an executive manager in a large resort hotel. "Or at least it seems that way, because you don't expect it from a woman. When my female boss comes down the hall the walls shake and employees quake. Screw up once, you're warned, loud. Screw up twice, and you're dead. Flexible hours to accommodate infant care—forget it. She'd laugh in your face. Yes, she runs a great hotel, and believe me, there aren't very many women with a job like hers. But she goes for the burn."

It has been an article of feminist faith that women in positions of power would have a positive effect on the fortunes of women lower down the ladder. But women in pursuit of success can also be caught up in competitive behavior. They may be forced to look out for number one whether they intend to or not. More than one woman said that to protect her career she had to be careful about helping other women.

ELEANOR, class of '74, head of film development for a professional education agency: "It's my job to hire producers and production companies to carry out educational film projects. I have to be careful about being too female-oriented. I was giving a lot of work to female producers, and got the feeling that my boss saw it as a weakness. Now, I make sure for every project I give a woman, I give two to a male producer."

When upper-level jobs did open up, support from the top brass was usually so feeble that women positioned for promotion didn't always grasp the opportunity.

EILEEN: "When my boss was promoted, I should have been a top contender for his job. But I looked at it and said, 'There's no way I'm going to go for this.' It was even more demanding timewise: I was pregnant with my first child, and I had reached an age where I was no longer willing to sell my whole life to the company."

Eileen's predicament echoes what many other women told us: the *system* itself needs changing, rather than the women within the system adapting to its often rigid demands:

"I talked about this with certain other women in my company. Some would have been more willing than I to take on the job, but they said there was a glass ceiling and no woman could realistically compete for the job anyway. Getting through the selection process was virtually impossible. At the next level, there were no women at all."

We asked Eileen if she might have competed for the job if there had been more women at the level above her. "It would have made a difference, yes. I'm making it sound worse than it was. There were some excellent role models in other divisions of the company. I worked for a good VP, a man who respected what I brought to the table. He shared the information that he should, because he wanted me to be effective. He didn't lock me out. But I would never have had the close personal relationship with him that his male regional sales managers had."

ROLE MODELS, MENTORS, AND NETWORKS

Often, as they advance in their professions, women feel that they must "do it alone." Some Hunter women rejected any need to reach out for a helping hand. A 1950s graduate who is an executive in a large accounting company affirms: "I have done it alone by believing in me!"

Another graduate from the 1940s, who is vice president of an architectural firm, agreed. "I made it without help. If you are bright enough and persevere, nothing or no one can stop you."

There's no argument that strong motivation and determination are crucial to success in any field. Yet few climb to the very top without the approval and support of people upstairs. Hunter women across the century said that beyond their parents and teachers they had few professional role models to emulate. For the most part, mentors for women, where they exist, are still largely male.

SANDRA, class of '70, described an observation she had made: "I belong to a Women in Science organization. Every year they honor women who are first-rate. These are exceptional women in their sixties and seventies—they all have complete, wonderful lives—huge careers, families, children.

"Over the years, I've tried to analyze what they had in common. The only thing I could pin down is that all of them said they had great relationships with their fathers and they all had male mentors. Now, they had all been through the same stuff in high school that we all went through—the guidance counselors all told them they should never go into science. But their fathers had said to them, 'So what if they don't want you, you go anyway. You can do it.'

"They expected approval from men and it was natural to them to find a male mentor. Their fathers had given them their complete approval, so they didn't need to please the world."

Mentors, either male or female, present certain dangers for women already vulnerable to pleasing others as a way of life. Mentors often expect their protégés to assume their values and enter into a hierarchical relationship. For women trying to break out and find a sense of personal identity, following a mentor may seem like submissiveness.

Male mentors may also give a sexual edge to the relationship or, more often, a paternal one. Several Hunter women told us that their relationship with their male or female mentors tended to duplicate their relationship with their mother or father.

EMILY, class of '77: "It's confusing, because if you break away from your mentor it seems like you're being disloyal to your parent. When I wanted to move up in my job, I found myself trapped. My boss loved me, but he wanted to keep me in my place. It exactly reflected the relationship I had with my father. I tried to please my boss as I did my parents. I saw quitting as the only way out of the relationship."

This was a theme we heard repeated several times. The workplace, where issues of power and control are constantly played out, is a likely culture for unresolved family problems to fester and burgeon. Good girls who have never completely worked out their independence from their parents are especially vulnerable.

In the end, mentoring is vital to women who wish to step into leadership. A critical mass of women in influential positions, willing to reinforce one another's decisions, to have the votes when they count, is far more effective than merely telling women to be more assertive.

Although most women have had little training in professional mentoring, they do have considerable experience in the hallmarks of good mentoring: nurturing, teaching, and friendship. The more difficult tasks of mentoring—defining expectations, setting goals, teaching strategic thinking—are also part of a woman's life experience.

Mentoring among women is closely related to that overused term, networking. Grace, a senior copy writer and vice president of a medical advertising agency, said that she never understood what networking could be—or how much she needed it—until she ran into a serious problem at work.

GRACE, class of '68: "At my shop, anxiety radiates from the top. The president of the agency, who came from the medical side of the business, is just a disaster in human relations. But Max is a friend of my family; he started me in the business, trained me, and promoted me. He treats me, personally, very well, except that he underpays me by about twenty grand a year.

"My relationship with him is a carbon copy of my relationship with my father. I handle him. I know how to keep him from blowing his top. I hate this, but I can't help myself. It's the only job I've ever had, and somewhere in my head I'm convinced no one else would ever hire me.

"Lo and behold, a headhunter called me with a job offer from another, smaller agency. The boss is a woman, and she offered me twenty-five thousand dollars above my present salary and the chance to learn in new areas in which I'm lacking experience. I checked around with my friends in the industry, who said that it was a good move. I decided to break with Max and go for it.

"When I told Max I was leaving, he went crazy. He told me I was making the mistake of my life, that my career would be ruined. He said he had inside information and knew for a fact that the agency was on its way down the drain and that I was about to enter the fires of hell if I went with this woman. He said he would give me anything I wanted if I would stay.

"I panicked. I had never taken such a huge leap before—let's face it, I had never even changed jobs before. I got in touch with a writer who knew all the agencies inside-out, knew all the players, including my boss. She reassured me that the new agency was solvent and stable, that the president and creative staff were tough, but great to work with.

"I don't know if that's networking or mentoring or what. Max tormented and threatened me right up to the last day. But this writer, a woman, counseled me through the whole process of decision-making. Can you imagine if women had that kind of cooperation at the top?"

BREAKING THROUGH

Attaining leadership means making choices, staying visible, taking responsibililty for your own success, and being willing to compete and pay the price.

From talking with the Hunter women we isolated several factors that seemed to block women from the top. First, they didn't see themselves in leadership roles. Second, they were ambivalent about jockeying for positions of power, playing company politics, and putting themselves forward. Third was isolation. Even if a woman can get into a top slot, she was likely to be the only woman there; she did not have enough support from a community of peers to successfully do the job. Finally, women said they were locked out of the top jobs.

EILEEN: "You've got to face the fact that there is something actively negative working against you from the other side. From the male members of the staff, there is no welcome."

According to Elizabeth Dole, speaking as Secretary of Labor, "There can be little doubt that a woman or minority, no matter how well schooled, what their age, or how thick their portfolio, enters many business organizations with limited or no hope of reaching the top."

Current statistics bear her out. In 1991, *Fortune* magazine counted four thousand corporate heads and found that only nineteen were women. Similar percentages are seen at the top of virtually every profession, from government to law to engineering.

One statistic applies to all areas of work: Women still earn sixty-six cents to every dollar earned by a man. *Newsweek*: "The wage gap has narrowed by less than a dime over the last two decades. The higher women advance, the larger the wage gap."

When we asked "What do you think needs to happen to make leadership more viable?" a few women, including Emily and Sharon, said they believed it was just a matter of time.

EMILY, class of '77: "I think a few more women will make it up there, and they will open the doors."

SHARON, class of '73: "When you get a larger number of qualified women in the pipeline, that's the way connections are made. Women are getting there. In finance, we're doing billion-dollar deals, just like men. Where the network gets big enough, some will push up to the top."

Several other women sharply disagreed. Lauren: "We've got to get back in their face and stir things up."

EILEEN, class of '72, believes that opportunities will be increased only when companies begin to appreciate the benefits of hiring women and minorities. "Instead of simply hiring in their own image—whites hire whites, men hire men—companies should actively offer equal employment opportunities to all kinds of people. Diversity is tough to accomplish because you're dealing with basic human nature in terms of people's comfort level."

RENEE, one of the few women in our study to become CEO of a large company: "When I first became president and CEO of my firm, the women were all paid substantially less, and they were conditioned to think they should not ever be paid more. I changed that, but I had to wait until I was in a position of power and knew what to demand."

In her role as CEO, Renee has consciously decided not to follow male stereotypes. "To me, acting like a man in business means using the techniques that oppress, encourage competition among employees—that style obliterates the highest level of contributions that women can bring to the top ranks."

ROXANNE, class of '43: "Women need a sense that their own female identity is worthy of respect and emulation. Instead of identifying with men when they get power, women should be more articulate about their own strengths. Otherwise, we're just going to see women acting like men and repeating the same mistakes men make."

As a more rapid and certain way of reaching positions where they are in control, many women are opting to go into business on their own. Some business experts believe that entrepreneurship is the wave of the future for women. Yet women who drop out of the system will miss the opportunity to bring change for future generations of women.

By contrast, Emily said she loved the atmosphere and challenge of a big corporation. "You can't get that if you start your own company. I wasn't able to maneuver up in my first job, but I want to get into a different field, maybe film production. Sherry Lansing did it at Twentieth Century–Fox, God knows how. I think I could do it, too."

EIGHT

LOVE AND MARRIAGE

The man I chose to marry in my twenties is not the same man I would choose now.

—EMILY, *class of '77*

There was a tendency among many Hunter women who had been brilliant achievers in school and successful in work to accept second-class status in their love relationships. We wondered why they had difficulty translating their academic and professional achievements into the area of emotions.

When we looked at this pattern against the larger perspective of their lives a distinct picture emerged. Bright women learn to become independent at an early age. They easily sense the expectations of adults who want them to shine, and act *as if* they are more self-sufficient than they are. Underneath this exterior, they still maintain a strong need for approval, a need they transfer into adult relationships. This duality was exemplified in the lives of the Hunter women across the century. Being smart did not seem to noticeably help them when it came to finding love. To the contrary, there was evidence that intelligence posed unique problems.

WOMEN IN LOVE

Surprisingly, throughout the century, smart women tended to ingore intelligence as a factor in measuring a man's suitability as a partner. They selected mates based on stability, and often chose men whose professions and careers they could be proud of and "stand behind."

Back in the 1920s, 83 percent of the Hunter women said they had trouble being viewed as both feminine and intelligent. Most coped by simply damping down the intelligence factor and fulfilling the expectations of their times for femininity. The majority said they were "happily married." Several described the anguish of facing widowhood after forty years or more of marriage. Rachel, class of '11, was typical: "I try to hold on to fifty-five beautiful years together. One night, not long before my husband died, neither of us knew his death was immiment. I was already in bed and he sat down beside me and said what a good life we had had together. I hold on to that." For the most part the older graduates said they were happy in their relationships—but at the expense of developing professional lives.

In the mid-age range we saw many more divorces coinciding with the burgeoning women's movement. Several women told us that their marriages broke up when they began to develop their abilities and pursue more challenging careers.

Among younger women of the 1970s and 1980s, some were married, some expected to marry in the future, and some were determined to remain single. When it came to intimate relationships, 67 percent of the Hunter women said being intelligent still created a problem for them. In an era when women are expected to achieve in the larger world, coping with feminine versus smart is not as simple as it used to be.

A 1929 graduate painted this cynical picture of modern smart women: "The brilliant, successful women of today may be financially successful, but if they're not married before age twenty-five, they have a tough time. Men fear and resent them. The streetwise gals, not big on intellectual matters, use sex wisely and get more out of life, while the poor superwomen have to put up with an exorbitant amount of nonsense. If your personality is strong and you have a sense of humor, you may be able to survive."

ROSEMARIE, class of '69: "It's been difficult to find a partner who's not emotionally threatened by me. Most people think I'm intimidating. People have said this about me since I was sixteen. I'm trying to combat this impression. I'd like to find someone who's not threatened by me, who wants to discuss things, relationships, the 'you and me' part of life. Most men are still uncomfortable with this."

The Hunter women told us men hadn't changed much, at least not deep down. A 1963 grad: "My husband probably wishes I weren't a doctor. I know he'd rather have me take care of him and pay less attention to my own needs. He's not threatened because I'm smarter than he is, but because I have my own desires and I'm acting on them."

SANDRA, class of '70, a research biologist at a large eastern university, had a different take on modern relationships: "If you're a man, your excellence and achievement enhance your masculinity. If you're a woman, they don't enhance your femininity. The more successful a man is, the more he's respected at work, the more appealing he is on the marriage market. I know I sound bitter, but that's how it's been for me. I think we have to imagine women in a different way."

SHARON, class of '73, agreed that being smart might be a problem for some women, but not for her: "I never felt men wouldn't like me because I was smart. I've done significant work, and I want my husband to do the same and to appreciate me and my talents."

Recent surveys of young, unmarried men support their contention that men enjoy dating and marrying accomplished women. A recent national poll reported by *Time* magazine found that 86 percent of the young men surveyed said they were looking for a spouse who was ambitious and hardworking; "an astonishing 48 percent expressed an interest in staying home with their children."

Not surprisingly, however, several young Hunter women spoke of the "lack of commitment syndrome" of the modern male.

JOYCE, class of '82, thought the noticeable unwillingness of eligible men to make a marital commitment was due to something fundamental in their makeup: "Men my age don't feel the biological clock tick the way women do. They can concentrate on careers or education or whatever, and put relationships on the back burner almost indefinitely. Men think, 'I'm not going to do it today, so why think about it?' When they're ready, they know they can reach out and someone will be there.

"My boyfriend's very focused and can't seem to look at too many things at once. I want to say to him, 'Take the party hat off your head. Let's get married.' Yet I don't. I'm afraid I might lose him if I give him an ultimatum. Let's face it, there aren't too many good men around. But the world seems full of smart, fabulous, single women with good jobs."

The Hunter women were guarded when it came to openly discussing sexuality. The older women barely mentioned sex; the younger women were surprisingly practical about it.

CYNTHIA, said that when it came to sex, the important thing to her was self-control:

"In the 1960s, there was no sexual revolution for me. I had a lot of heavy making-out experiences in college, but certainly not in high school. I decided not to have sex until the New York State abortion law went into effect, because I wasn't going to ruin my life over something that is irrevocable. I have always been rather smugly proud of that. The law made abortion safe, affordable, accessible. I made a very self-determining decision and I made it entirely by myself.

"When I did choose to become sexually active, I was always careful, so in my case pregnancy never developed as an issue. I had been involved with people emotionally, and I've always been definite about what I was and was not going to do. I never felt I had to have sex just because a man wanted me to."

Most of the women were not as calculating as Cynthia, although as a group they appeared to be, once again, "good girls." Most reported that they did not have sexual intercourse in high school, many experimented in college, and most married and said they confined their sexuality within the frame of a monogamous relationship. Their hesitancy to discuss their sexual feelings openly made any definite conclusions difficult to draw.

A WOMAN'S INDEPENDENCE

In the not-too-distant past, women were inclined to measure their own success by the success of the men they married. Direct action on their own behalf was unfamiliar. Women were famous for pulling the strings in the background while making their men look like the brains and breadwinners. Many older Hunter women described this process, although even in retrospect they often insisted that this was positive behavior that enhanced their married life.

Money played an integral part in the way the Hunter women viewed both success and independence. Seventy-one percent of all women in our study equated "success" with financial independence. When it came to relationships, however, money was seldom mentioned by most of the older women, except to note that they had married financially successful men. Many still clung to the belief that handling money is a man's job. They avoided taking responsibility for their financial well-being, and attributed financial success to their husband's endeavors.

All of the younger women who graduated after the 1950s said that money was an important factor in their relationships. Several spoke vehemently on the subject. Some had made serious mistakes in their first marriages that had left them financially stranded later on, when the marriage ended.

SHARON, class of '73, believes that egalitarian relationships are only possible if both partners make equal financial contributions. "My advice to young women is to get yourself in a position to support yourself so you're not dependent on someone else for either your self-esteem or your life-style. My sister works, but she depends on her husband socially and financially. If her husband ever walks out on her, everything will collapse. You can't find your own identity through another person. And you can't view a relationship as your salvation."

RENEE, class of '57, learned the hard way what can happen when a woman doesn't have her own financial resources. "My mother was a very successful career women in the 1940s and '50s, but as a child I wanted her to be a housewife. So when it came time for me to marry and have a family, my immediate inclination was to avoid following in her footsteps. I majored in philosophy in college, but didn't have any professional aspirations. I thought I would eventually do something, but it didn't seem important to figure out what."

Renee married a young college instructor, and began work toward an advanced degree so she might also teach on the college level. "I gave up that idea. Although my husband's salary was very low, he was on a career path and his work seemed more important than mine. I got a job as an editorial assistant to help support us while he carried out his plan.

"Actually, I liked my job on the magazine very much. Then my husband had an opportunity to teach for a year on the West Coast, so I quit work and went with him. We had a baby. When we returned to New York, I had a fellowship to Columbia graduate school, but found it impossible to keep up. We had no extra money for a baby-sitter, and my husband had no interest in domestic chores or child care. I had another baby.

"With two small children, I got a part-time job, so I could supplement our income. I thought this was a good compromise. I expected to work—after all, I had a working mother, and it was the 1960s, and women were expected to contribute financially. I didn't consider it an option to work full-time or try to develop a career. I wanted to be with my children.

"From that point on, I had a very sad, difficult time. I commuted from the suburbs to my job in Manhattan. My husband grew very distant, and began drinking heavily. Alcoholism took over his life. Our marriage declined and then just seemed to evaporate."

We asked Renee how she had faced this critical choice point in her life. "I explored every possible avenue to keep my family together, but all I could do was perpetuate a hopeless situation. I cried every single morning between 5 A.M. and 6 A.M., terrified that if I left my husband I would be unable to support the kids by myself.

"When you're in a desperate situation, at some point you decide that you're just not going any further downhill. You grab for a rope and you just hold on. In my case, it was clear that I had to get out of the marriage, but I was afraid of the future. My mother was there for me to talk to. And my women friends were enormously helpful in offering emotional support, as well as concrete advice about the process of separation and looking for a better job. I don't think I could have made it through it all without them."

Divorce is devastating to the woman who must look after her children and also try to enter a tough job market.

RENEE: "When I entered the job market full-time, I had to struggle to catch up. I didn't have the right credentials or the right kind of experience for a first-rate job. I was thirty-four years old, and I had to start at entry level. I remember how exhausting and frustrating it was for me to try to do it all without any help."

Renee landed a job in market research, and later went into advertising. She discovered that she had the makings of an excellent account executive, able to bring in clients and develop new business at a remarkable rate. Ultimately, she worked her way up to president and eventually CEO of her own agency. "I did follow in my mother's footsteps—it just took me a long time to do it, and by waiting so long I made it much harder than it had to be.

"I'm fifty-three now. Five years from now I would like to retire. I hope that I've done the right kind of retirement planning so that I have a comfortable margin. I don't require luxury. I'd like to keep on working in some way, perhaps another field, perhaps volunteer work or consulting.

"I've told my daughters over and over that they should always be prepared to pay their own way and be confident enough not to depend on anyone else. I want my girls to be self-sufficient first— and everything else second."

Renee's own lessons had been so harshly taught that she now believes she may have passed on the message of independence too rigorously. "My older daughter is angry with me today. She says she wishes she had chosen a husband who could take care of her. She's stressed out with responsibilities and blames me.

"I know sometimes you long for someone else to come along and take up the burden. I've felt that way myself."

A few young Hunter women expressed the same sentiments as Renee's daughter. This falling back toward the old-style marriage where the man earned the dominant income was a whisper in our study, not loud enough to be called a trend. It seemed to come from the young women in their twenties and early thirties who were in very demanding careers and also trying to raise children. Their plea for help seemed to come from an overload of pressures and responsibilities.

DIVISION OF LABOR

Next to money, the single biggest source of resentment in women's lives are men who don't pitch in at home. A nationwide Roper poll of three thousand women reported in 1991 that the more women work side by side with men, at home and on the job, the less they seem to like them and the more angry they become.

EILEEN, class of '72, said that couples get into doing "what they're good at." "It just happens that he's good at running errands and I'm good at cleaning the bathroom, shopping, cooking for guests. Women are grateful for whatever men are willing to do around the house. I bite my tongue whenever I catch myself thanking him for putting the dishes in the dishwasher. Why should I thank him?"

For some women, home is a "calling," a place where they best express their intelligence and their talents. Men almost never view domestic tasks as self-expression. Most men, the Hunter women said, confine their responsibilities to "external maintenance." "I don't know why," said Kitty, class of '33, "but my husband does the outside, I do the inside."

ROXANNE, class of '43: "Face it. The truth is, if you marry you get a second job; the opposite is true for men."

Issues surrounding marriage and relationships—particularly division of labor, work, and social roles—revolve around power. Power can be defined as the control of resources which allow one person to get others to behave differently than they might want to. Few would deny that the average man possesses more power than a woman, and that his power extends into private relationships.

Changing the balance of power threatens the most sacred areas of everyday life. Many women are as hesitant to grasp power as most men are hesitant to give it up. Each may fear that if a woman gains power, a man may lose it.

Our society generally does not look at the power status of women and men as one unit. Rather, if a woman has power, her mate is often viewed as weak, and vice versa. In our culture, equal power-sharing is somehow alien and threatening to the status quo. Many women are more comfortable seeking power in a nonconfrontational, manipulative way.

EMILY, class of '77, used a modern kind of manipulation to gain power in her marriage. "I had always felt that my husband was smarter and more creative than I am, although he doesn't earn much money. I'm the big earner, because I'm a compulsive worker and I hustle. Making more money gives me a terrific sense of control, which I wield like a warrior. But the money thing has created enormous tension between us, because deep down I resent the fact that he doesn't contribute equally. I've also learned in the last ten years that I'm every bit as smart as he is. Our whole relationship seems like a pack of lies. We're trying to work it out, but the truth is, the man I chose to marry in my twenties is not the same man I would choose now."

Hopefully, it has become ancient history for intelligent and capable women to view fulfillment as having married successful men who will shower them with their abundance. Even so, the choices women make come with a price tag. Women who reject traditional roles must cope with the resistance and downright disapproval of others—perhaps their parents and relatives, perhaps their colleagues and friends. They also have to put aside their internalized critic that cautions them to conform and blend in.

The threat of divorce, conflict over time to serve both family and careers, and finding a mate who appreciates and values their intelligence—all go into the choice of relationships.

ROXANNE, class of '43: "Anyone who has ever been married or in a long-term relationship knows that they are always in a process of changing. You always lose something of yourself in marriage. It's a matter of degree—when your gain outweighs your loss, you're in great shape."

CHOOSING SINGLEHOOD

More than 25 percent of the women in our study chose to remain single. They viewed mates and children as viable options, not preordained destinies. A woman who chooses not to marry may be cast by friends and colleagues into the "lonely spinster" category, the "selfish, career-oriented" role, or the "desperate predator." It's not always easy for a woman—*single by choice*—to ignore the social pressures to marry.

"People really think there's something wrong with you if you're not married," said Lee, who graduated from Hunter in 1951. "About ten years ago I went for a job as a sales rep—a field I had a good track record in. The male interviewer asked me why I had never married. He seemed perplexed when I told him I did not consider marriage a part of my future. I didn't get the job, and I'm certain it was because my value system didn't match his. I get furious now when I realize that I let him get away with that question."

The Hunter women who chose to remain single were adamant that others recognize their lifestyle as their own choice. Rosemarie, class of '69: "A lot of people think if you're not married it's because nobody ever asked you, the worst thing in the world from society's viewpoint."

Rosemarie is currently in a monogamous relationship, but has no plans to marry. She worries that marriage might engulf her, forcing her to meet the needs of others at the sacrifice of her own life and career. "I was brought up by a single mother who had to struggle every day to take care of me. I saw her life as a sacrifice for me. I know I don't want a conventional marriage, and I can't envision a marriage where the husband shares equal responsibility for children and home. So I prefer none at all."

SHARON, class of '73, is also irritated by the assumptions that others make about her singlehood. "My life-style is hard for people to understand. I don't want what my colleagues at work want—the spouse and the two kids in the country every weekend. It's not for me. People say I'm sacrificing personal life to my career—that's their problem. I just never cared whether I was married or not. My friends analyze a statement like that for hours. But I like my independence. It feels good."

Women who choose to live without a "significant" identifiable partner said their social lives were sometimes curtailed. Helene, class of '62, who is divorced, said she would remarry only when she finds exactly the right partner. "Until then, I'm much happier on my own. The hard part is that the world is created by couples. The seductive scenes of family and home put a single woman outside the circle. Society says you're just treading water until you get a guy, no matter how satisfied you feel with your life. I resent the pressure and exclusion I feel for my present choice, which is to go it alone. My married friends are eager for me to get on with it again. I feel some subtle form of control is at work that I need to resist."

LEE, class of '51, was one of several women in our study who had remained unmarried because of her sexual preference, although she has a long-term committed relationship with another woman. "In high-school, I felt like two different people, trying to act like everybody else, but knowing inside I felt so different.

"I tried to talk to a counselor who was all warm and reassuring, offering good-natured admonition, but she could never say the word 'gay,' or God forbid, 'lesbian!' What I'm saying is, here I had these weird feelings for women, and I knew I was bright, I was getting this first-class education, but how in the hell was I going to be successful and homosexual? Nobody could tell me that."

Lee grew up as an outsider. She learned to hide her feelings and tried to blend in with other teenagers. Eventually, after some wrong choices along the way, she found the right partner and her place in the world.

"In many ways I lead a conventional, single life. Even by my own definition, I'm successful. I'm national sales manager of a manufacturing firm. I'm not a wife or mother, but I have a loving partner who has a successful career of her own. We share a lot, travel a lot, have friends in common.

"There have been the usual glitches along the way. Arguments about work, money, sex—the things I hear most couples argue about. The difference is that when I have relationship problems I don't have anyone to talk to. Socializing at work is difficult, too. There is still prejudice afoot."

Homosexual women remain America's invisible women. According to current statistics, there are an estimated 6 million to 13 million lesbians in the United States, most fully integrated into mainstream American life. Even though Lee is guarded with us when she talks about her choice of life-style, she says that the activism of women's and gay groups speaking out about sexuality has helped her become more outspoken. "I want to be free to let people know who I am, like everyone else."

•

Rosemarie, Sharon, Helene, and Lee represent a new and growing trend—women who have chosen to postpone marriage or not to marry at all. In our study, 65 percent from the 1970s have never married. In the general population, 8 million American women in their late twenties have never married.

Nor did every woman in our study expect to have children, again reflecting a national trend for American women to forego motherhood. The Hunter women in the 1940s and '50s had larger families than women of any other decade. In the 1960s, no Hunter woman had more than three children. It's difficult to predict the trend for women of the '70s and '80s, because they are still young enough to have additional children.

SHARON, class of '73: "I want to have fulfilling relationships with men, but not marriage and children. In my case, having a child would be going against my instincts."

LAUREN, class of '76: "My husband would like to have children, but the truth is, I know I'm not cut out for it. I'm driven, obsessive about work—I lack the mothering instinct."

Even today, their statements take a certain degree of courage. It's not easy for a single woman to steer her own course and ignore the social pressure to marry. Psychologist and researcher Lawrence Kutner summed up the negative attitudes that confront childless women: "[They are] sometimes viewed with suspicion and disdain. They may be accused of being self-centered and uncaring . . . Yet, research on childless couples shows that, on the whole, people who are childless by choice report being more happily married."

Sharon and Lauren have made a clear choice. By no means did they speak for all of contemporary Hunter women, most of whom still expect to marry and have families. Joyce, a 1982 graduate, said that she had a strong desire to have children. "It's the one thing I want most. I want to be a mother. My problem is finding a man who wants to get married."

CYNTHIA, class of '67, also hopes to have children, and would like to somehow re-create for them the special childhood experiences she shared with her own mother. "I'd like to have a daughter. I don't think I'd do as well with little boys. But if I had a son, he'd be a Hunter boy. When my friends have had children, we say, 'Oh, a Hunter girl,' because she's so bright. I'd like to say that about my own daughter."

NINE

BALANCING ACTS

How can a woman have her mind on a career
when her two-year-old is home with a high fever?

— *KITTY, class of '33*

One problem that continues to stymie women determined to reach the top is the emotionally charged issue of how to handle a high-pressure job and at the same time adequately nurture a family.

We know that men's career paths can be charted like super-highways, with signposts marking distinct hierarchical stages—from exploration and education, through recognition and advancement, capped by maintenance and eventual retirement. Women's career paths, by comparison, seem like meandering country lanes, changing direction to meet the needs of the territory and frequently side-tracked by the barriers they encounter. The Hunter graduates confirmed that women take varied paths in career development and tend to have many interruptions and digressions.

Our data show that trying to balance home, children, work, and economic demands remains the most difficult problem for women of any age. A multitude of experts and opinion-makers are ready to give advice on how to juggle careers and family relationships. Their recommendations are categorized in three ways: 1) choose one and let the other go; 2) do both but realize that you cannot do either well; 3) keep trying, until you manage to earn an "A" in both.

The assumption throughout seems to be that it is exclusively the women's responsibility to solve the dilemma. The subtext suggests that if a woman applies herself properly, she will discover the magic solution and make everything fit together.

As HELENE, class of '62, says, "I fell for the line that if I tried hard enough I could be a superwife, supermom, superlover, supercook, and a superknockout—all in one, all the time—just by slipping from one role into another, slipping from a negligee into a business suit. I learned to discard that sort of nutty thinking and set some priorities. But I had to give up all that approval from everyone. I had to let some people down and live with the fact that they found me less than perfect. It's hard to adopt an 'I-don't-give-a-damn attitude' at my age, but I'm trying."

PHYLLIS, class of '58, is vehement: "The burden to make things work seems to be on women. It's as if I'm out of step if I expect anyone else to change."

RENEE put it succinctly: "Women want to work and they also want to have children. How they're supposed to do both at once remains a mystery."

The conflict between career and family life is not new to modern women; it plagued our Hunter women throughout the century, and they dealt with it according to the mores of their time. For most of the older women, there was no question about which came first. Peggy, class of '37, realized that the women of her generation were caught between the old tradition of being a homemaker and the need to be someone in her own right. "I decided to stay home when I had kids. I don't regret the choice. My kids have benefited from my intellect and education, which hired help could not have provided. I made the decision myself. But I think if I had it to do again, my choice would be different."

KITTY, class of '33, also chose to stay home, although she says her choice was largely based on her husband's perception of family life. "We never considered any other option. How can a woman have her mind on a career when her two-year-old is home with a high fever?"

RENEE, class of '57, bitterly disagreed. "I went that route, and let me tell you, the kid gets over the fever. Two days later it's all forgotten. But that job is gone. And if you wait until your kids are, what, ten or eleven years old? Then you're ten years older in a marketplace that adores youth. Where is the career for that loving Mommy who sat at the bedside?"

CAROLE, class of '54: "The women of my generation have led two lives—pre– and post–Betty Friedan. The first half of my adult life was very different from the second half. I was a housewife for twelve years. When my youngest child started school, I took an entry-level job as a lab technician. I climbed through the ranks until I earned a senior staff position. It took seventeen years. I'm the only person to make it to this level without a Ph.D. I tried to go to graduate school, but I had the house, the kids, and an ailing parent to care for—it was more than I could physically handle. Now, the kids are out of the nest, but I'm too tired to go back to school. Some things you just have to let go."

HELENE, class of '62, wonders if it isn't mostly about money. "Basically, we all need to be able to afford full-time help we can feel secure with, so we can do our jobs to the fullest potential. We need to respect whoever is the full-time helper, pay them enough to do the job with some amount of commitment. Staying home with kids is not playtime, not if you do it right."

RENEE, class of '57: "I don't think the consciousness of men has changed enough to make life easier for women. Maybe a few corporations have qualified day-care centers, with an open pock-etbook and a loving heart. But most of the country still has mothers trying to figure out how to go to work and take care of their kids at the same time."

Emily, a young mother who graduated from Hunter in 1977, has recently quit her job to stay home with her two small children. She believes she is going back to the traditional way of doing things, unaware that in fact, throughout this century, the majority of mothers in America, especially those in the lower economic strata, have always worked and have had to face the stress of balancing their jobs with raising children.

OUT OF THE PAST

The oldest of the Hunter women that we personally interviewed, the 1914 graduate, has seen it all and knows the score. "Women have always been expected to be mothers and also do everything else, including hold down jobs. That's not news and it hasn't changed that much."

Regina was born in 1898 on Manhattan's Upper East Side. Her house at 101st Street and Madison Avenue is now the site of Mount Sinai Hospital. When she was still a toddler, the family moved farther north, to 143rd Street. "I grew up in Harlem, but it was a different place in those days. Beautiful, safe—like living in the country."

Regina's grandparents were German immigrants who originally settled in South Carolina. "My mother was a real southern belle, very dependent. She always gave us a hot lunch at noon, always took my brother and me to picnics or to a play. I remember seeing Maude Adams in *Peter Pan* when I was quite small, and Nijinsky, too, in the ballet. My mother fostered in me a great love for the theater and culture. She was an educated woman, but that was as far as it went. She never spoke up at the dinner table, and the friends she had were wives of Father's friends."

An interminable bout of whooping cough kept Regina out of elementary school and at home under the doting eye of her parents. She recalls her father reading to her during long sleepless nights. "My father loved books and encouraged me to read. When I was ten years old I wrote a column for a child's magazine which he admired very much. He and I discussed Dickens, George Eliot, and many Russian writers he had read. I still have my father's books.

When I was thirteen he gave me the complete set of Mark Twain.
I still have those books, too."

At age eleven, Regina was determined to march with the suffragettes up Fifth Avenue. She set out on her own, without per-
mission from her parents, on a bright Saturday morning in 1910.
"Thousands of us gathered at Washington Square. At the head of
the parade was Inez Milholland riding a handsome white charger.
I carried a placard with 'Votes for Women' in huge letters. I've never
forgotten the feeling I had that morning—like the world belonged
to me, and I could do anything I wanted."

Regina's parents had prepared her well for her entrance into
Hunter that same year. She thrived there. "Being smart never both-
ered me. I was an excellent speaker on numerous topics. From the
age of twelve or thirteen, I was a regularly published author in
several religious and academic publications. I published an article
about the educator Julia Richman in *The American Hebrew* when
I was fifteen. My teachers encouraged all of my talents."

Regina enthusiastically entered Hunter College, where she majored in history and edited the college newspaper. She developed
an avid interest in botany and ornithology, and took long outings
in Central Park with her teachers. Her great loves—literature, nature, and public speaking—were shaped in these years.

Nevertheless, she recalled that her overriding goal was to marry
and have children. Ten days after college graduation she married
the young musician/sculptor she had met during a summer in New
England. They lived blissfully in the exuberant bohemian atmosphere of Greenwich Village in the 1920s. Regina remembers hearing
an emaciated Edna St. Vincent Millay read her unpublished poems
in a basement café; listening to George Gershwin and Oscar Levant
tearing up the piano until dawn in another Village hideaway. "I was
a companion to my husband. In that circle, I was an observer, not
a participant. I felt I didn't have much to offer."

Regina joined a charitable organization and went into the city's
worst neighborhoods, bringing medical aid to tubercular women.
This activity ended when she became pregnant with her first child.

During her pregnancy, Regina started a book club for young women, who would meet regularly at her Greenwich Village apartment to discuss current novels.

Regina's husband, Lou, contracted a progressive illness which was incurable. To stay busy and keep from worrying about his failing health, Regina accepted their rabbi's invitation to give a talk for a charitable fundraising event.

"It was my first adult speaking engagement. It distracted me from my worries, but I didn't think about a career as a public speaker. I was much too busy coping with the mounting problems. A sick, demanding, frightened husband who needed my constant presence. Three healthy children filled with energy and curiosity. Those years were turmoil, constantly trying to nurse him and mother them."

A fire in his studio destroyed her husband's work, and doubtless sapped whatever will to live he possessed. At age thirty-one Regina found herself widowed, with three small boys, in the midst of the Great Depression. "We lost our house because I couldn't raise the mortgage money. I told myself that Lou was away on a long trip and would be home soon. I just couldn't cope."

Her sons stayed with relatives and foster parents while Regina retreated to her aunts' home and gave in to her grief. With her parents' help she found a small apartment in the suburbs. She gathered her sons together and started to look for work.

She took a job as a camp counselor so that her boys would have as good a vacation as their schoolmates. When one of the neighborhood mothers organized a rotating child-care nursery, Regina worked part-time for the public library. She quickly realized she could never make ends meet with small, fill-in jobs.

In the depths of the Depression, there were few jobs for men, and even fewer for women. Families were on relief; mothers stood for hours in breadlines to feed their children. Nevertheless—with no role models, no community of women to inform her or ease her way, no friends to turn to for help or encouragement—Regina went job-hunting. Unable to find a job, she was creative enough to invent her own career. In the early years of her marriage, Regina had completed her master's degree in speech. She continued working part-time and also began to give book lectures. With book clubs gaining in popularity, Regina soon became a sought-after guest speaker. Her talent for extemporaneous speaking, her educational background, her fine critical sense, and her gift of total recall—she could remember anecdotes and quote authors endlessly—made her a natural.

Children often see their mother's work as a competitive and depriving force, taking away their parent with no compensation to themselves. However, Regina's sons were proud of her public appearances. She was charming, witty, and friendly, and their friends admired her. Gaining confidence as both parent and lecturer, Regina began to socialize again. She met a recently divorced physician and, "after I convinced myself that he would be the perfect husband and father, I married him." The marriage never brought the family unity she sought. Shortly after World War II ended, Regina's second husband left her, admitting that he had had countless affairs, as well as an illegitimate child, during their twelve years together.

Regina was now head of the Speakers Bureau for a national charitable foundation, with responsibility for booking speakers across the country. She also had a second successful career as a book and theater reviewer for a newspaper. Yet the effect of the failure of her marriage was devastating.

"I was almost fifty years old, and I had to start all over again. Thankfully, I had many friends who kept me busy socially."

She also applied herself to her work. Recognizing the need for leadership training for women, she created a Leadership Training Manual for the national board of the foundation for which she worked, and then conducted workshops across the country. She was invited to become a charter member of the United Nations Speakers Research Committee. Through its auspices, she toured Israel, one of the first Americans to visit after the war.

Regina eventually married for the third time; the man had been a close friend of her first husband. "I hoped to find in a husband friendship, affection, physical love, and compatibility. It was not like my first love in my early twenties, but he was steadfast and loving. I was the great romance of his life, and that was a nice thing to be. We were happy for twenty-four years, until he died."

Her sons, she says, "are the three jewels in my crown. Each is special and smart. The oldest is a doctor; my second son is a director and professor of dramatics. My youngest son floundered for a while until he met a young woman who helped him find himself. Now he's head of a large business."

Despite the fact that she had marched up Fifth Avenue with the suffragettes, Regina had been brought up at a time and in a culture that taught women to define themselves in terms of their roles as wife and mother. Necessity forced her to play other roles, at which she appears to have succeeded magnificently.

In later decades women would expect to combine work with motherhood. But society had not taught Regina those lessons. She learned them for herself. Left alone by the premature death of her husband, her instinct for survival forced her to go beyond the role of mother. However, it's likely that even if circumstances had not grasped her by the neck, a woman of her energies and intelligence would have discovered satisfying avenues for self-expression.

MODERN ANXIETIES

We saw a tendency for younger women in our study to want to abandon high-pressure jobs in favor of full-time motherhood. Cynthia, class of '67, a broadcast journalist: "I'm getting married soon. I don't know yet if I will stop my career if I have a child, but I will definitely cut back in some way. If I had the answers I'd package it and sell it. I had full-time, concentrated, absolute center-of-the universe mothering. I believe that's how it should be done."

The birth of a child puts a strain on what may, up until that moment, have been a successful marital arrangement, with both partners functioning in parallel ways. When a child is involved, the issues of who will provide care and how becomes an insistent reality. Deep-seated expectations of roles come into play. Eileen, class of '72, a top executive with a large food distribution company, recently quit her job to have a baby.

EILEEN: "Our decision to have a family had a lot to do with the ticking biological clock. Ken and I had been married for a long time. We had talked about having kids, but thought we'd wait until we really wanted them. I worked for a very demanding company. It was easy to get caught up in that, to become so focused on work that you didn't think about the rest of your life. I was obsessed with individual goals and accomplishments.

"When I had my annual checkup at age thirty-five, my physician said I should think about getting off the Pill. That surprised me; I didn't realize I was that old. Then my last grandparent died— the last person of that generation of our family. I started thinking about a broader picture, about things continuing.

"I noticed that several of my contemporaries in the company, women I respected in their careers, were having babies. Seeing their choices began to push me in that direction.

"Some who continued to work after they had babies, they were doing things with their kids that to me, in my heart, felt wrong. One was a woman I respected a great deal. Like me, she traveled extensively. She talked about catching 7 A.M. planes and getting home on a 10 P.M. flight three days later. She had two kids under three years of age and didn't see them for half the week. I just couldn't do that. Maybe it worked for her, but I knew I couldn't face that.

"All these pieces began to come together for me. It wasn't one thing—it was a clutch of separate things. We took a long vacation, disconnected from work, and took stock of our priorities. When you get out of the craziness of the day-to-day, shut down the noise level for a while, we could admit that, yes, we did want to start a family. If we were going to do that, I realized something had to go. So the job went. It was a very conscious choice."

Eileen comes from a conservative working-class family where her father worked and her mother stayed home. She had been brought up to achieve academically and be first in whatever she attempted.

"My parents were proud of me, and if Ken and I did things our own way, they tolerated it. But when it came to having children, my parents' values really kicked in.

"It was instilled in me before I could think—if you're a mother, your children are your priority. The idea of checking your baby at a day-care center when it's six weeks old just appalls me. The value set that I hold says that if you bring them into the world, you're responsible for them; you should nurture them, you should teach them, you should instill values in that child. I wasn't willing to turn that over to somebody else.

"When I quit work, the baby wasn't born yet. People asked me when I was coming back. I don't know yet. I'll figure it out when I get to it. The other value I hold is that if you're going to do anything, do it well, and that includes raising a family. If that's my priority, then that's how I need to dedicate my time."

EMILY, class of '77, also has chosen to stay home. "When I had my first baby I wanted to stay home, but I was afraid to because I felt getting my job was sheer luck and I'd never find another one if I had to go back to work.

"When the second baby came, I finally quit. I told myself, the job will always be there, but the children won't. I didn't want someone else shaping their personalities. That scares me—the thought that somebody else would make their imprint on my children."

When we asked Emily if she planned to go back to work, her answer surprised me: "Yes. I expect to go back and to go back at the corporate level. I like big business. I'd like to run my own show, but in a big company. I'm thinking now I'd like to work in the movie business as a producer. Talk about pie in the sky. There's hardly a woman visible there. Yet in my fantasies that's what I dream about. I'm learning a lot right now about myself."

•

These Hunter women seemed to fret most about depriving their children of their personal "imprint"—working while relegating the care of their children to a "stranger"—and so they were opting for quitting their career path and staying home. Yet research appears to show that youngsters whose mothers are out on the fast track are more successful than closely mothered children.

A new nationwide study of 573 first-, third-, and fifth-graders in thirty-eight states has shown that children of working mothers outscore the children of nonworking mothers in math and reading, and demonstrate "significantly higher" IQ scores. The five-year study, conducted by psychologist John Guidubaldi from Kent State University, also showed that children of working moms have a better attendance rate and are more self-reliant. Surprisingly, they also spend more time recreationally with their mothers.

Psychologist Lois W. Hoffman, of the University of Michigan, found that children of working mothers believe that women can be competent and are also more likely to reject traditional roles. "The effect is stronger for daughters than sons because daughters are more likely to choose their mothers as role models. These daughters have higher scores on social adjustment, school performance, and professional accomplishments."

Although a few Hunter women, like Roxanne and even Renee, said they had felt abandoned by their own working mothers, many more said their working mothers set an example for them, at least in retrospect. Renee: "I don't think I appreciated what my mother accomplished until I was much older."

It's hard to say whether Eileen and Emily's choice to drop out of the work force to raise their children represents a larger trend. New surveys show that most women do *not* quit jobs when they have babies. Like men, they usually quit in order to move on to another, better job. Only 7 percent of women surveyed in a recent national poll said they left their jobs to stay at home. It's interesting, also, that on follow-up calls both Eileen and Emily said they were planning to return to work sooner than expected, and both were seeking additional academic qualifications to expand their options in the job market.

It's obvious that working mothers are now the norm. Their roles have widened dramatically to include both home and work, while the range of roles men play has barely changed. The nurturing male is still part of a dreamy mythical tale. A working mother spends approximately 22.5 hours each week on housework and child care. Her husband spends 7.4 hours a week, just one hour more than husbands of nonworking women.

It is impossible for many parents to understand why their accomplished daughters fight so hard to maintain their professional integrity. Terry, another graduate from 1977, says: "My parents say, 'I know she's smart, but if she wants to have children she should stay home with that child. She has to make a choice.' They cannot fathom that the society itself might change. My parents think the society works all right. It is we, their daughters, who are acting up."

Women have been buffeted from the old days of the 1950s into the expanding 1960s, to the freedom frenzy of the 1970s, to the era of superwoman of the 1980s, to the downsizing of the 1990s. Restructuring the workplace—equally distributing duties between husband and wife, pushing for child care, flex time, parental leave, and other innovations—still remains a minefield.

For change to occur, it is essential that a balance between "superwoman" and "working father" occur—when parenthood, career achievement, and household functioning gain a semblance of parity for men and women.

• TEN •

REENTRY

*As I sat in that classroom all those years later,
I knew I was smarter than anybody there, and
had always been."*

— INGRID, *class of '53*

Midlife and beyond is feared as a loss of youth, a time for closing down. A host of challenges beset Hunter women in this age range. Their struggles were often heroic—nursing husbands and elderly parents through illnesses, coping with widowhood, supporting children emotionally and often financially. For the Hunter women, middle and late adulthood were often years of trial.

It was also a stage that promised resurgent powers and potential. Women in their fifties, sixties, and older often reclaimed their intellectual potential and forged new paths for themselves. Women who had, for one reason or another, put their own goals on the back burner often switched tracks at this age. Decisions made in youth were reevaluated, and many decided to change course and make new choices.

We found that these were years of surprising vivacity and achievement among the older Hunter women. Prodded by the ticking clock, bolstered by a mature sense of self, several women in our study began to explore the full measure of their talents in their late forties, fifties, and sixties. Often there was a real urgency to their pursuits. Ultimately, for all of its travails, midlife proved to be a time of renewal, a time for new challenges and new possibilities for growth.

Overall, there was plenty of evidence in our study that women did have a "growth spurt" after they passed the age markers of fifty or sixty. They started successful businesses, wrote books, traded one career for another; many went back to school and earned advanced degrees.

Alexandra, a musician/songwriter, class of '53, completed the score and libretto of a musical comedy at the age of fifty-five. "Now I'm trying to get the show produced. It's almost impossible for an unknown to get a musical produced—let alone a middle-aged woman. I should have tried this thirty years ago—but they would have laughed at me then too. So what's the difference? I'll do it, or die trying."

Women in this stage of life encountered several critical choice points and, for the first time in their lives, many saw those choices clearly. They often became aware that marriage had lost its luster, and they had to choose between trying to renew the relationship, accepting the status quo, or opting for divorce. In terms of work, two patterns emerged among our graduates: women who chose to enter the work force for the first time in a serious way; and women who changed the direction of their existing careers, sometimes embarking on completely new professions.

All the Hunter women who struck out on new paths said that they weren't sure they would have enough time to achieve their goals. In retrospect, most said they made the right choice, and that they had achieved even more than they thought possible.

Lee, a graduate from the early 1950s: "I didn't get started until after I had spent twenty boring years in a job I hated. The sales area, which I love, had been closed to women of my generation, but opened up in the mid-1970s. I started from scratch. Within two years I matched my old salary, and then just shot up to the top. I enjoy my work. I exceed my company's expectations. I earn a great deal of money. I have two houses, a sizable cash reserve, and my health. It feels great."

For women who had raised families, new success in work offset feelings of loss over the "empty nest." Yet it isn't always a smooth equation. Late recognition of her gifts may trigger a period of regret in a woman. And even at this stage of life, a woman may have to sustain disapproval from those who think she should act "grand-motherly," support her husband's retirement, or passively accept the limitations of age. A woman who decides to change a significant component of her life—*at any age*—also changes the dynamic of her personal relationships.

Several Hunter women in their fifties and sixties told us that career shifts and new successes in middle age had a negative impact on their marriages. In these instances, the dynamic of the marital relationship was too rigid to accommodate individual growth. The most common scenario was that a woman expanded her life while her husband remained the same. Their goals and needs clashed, and the impact heightened the divorce potential. Husbands, ac-customed to being the primary trophy winner, often withdrew from their wives. This is a vulnerable age for a woman living in a culture that treasures youth; she may find herself battling dual problems of reentry into the work force and rejection at home.

A NEW LIFE

When Roxanne decided to expand her horizons, she discovered a basic flaw in her marriage. She had graduated from Hunter High in 1943, her childhood and adolescence marked by the Great Depression. The values of her working mother were that it was good for girls to be educated and to work, but that boys were inherently more important. "In our household, my brother was the one who was idealized and pampered. Mother expected me to get good grades in school, but that wasn't considered anything special."

Abiding by the expectations of her family, Roxanne went to Hunter College, and became an elementary school teacher. She married a psychotherapist and raised one child, a daughter. Her husband and child, she said, were the core of her world. She treated her husband the way her mother had treated her brother. "He always came first. I was happy to admire and support him in everything he wanted to do. I didn't realize then that if he was always first, I was always second. The same way I had been with my brother."

Roxanne continued teaching elementary school for twenty-four years. "Eventually, I suffered from teacher burnout, and yet I was afraid to quit working. I had seen my mother deteriorate when she retired; her self-esteem began to erode and her intellectual skills were severely impaired. I didn't want that to happen to me. Also, although I enjoyed being a mother, my daughter was grown. I was in a quandary of how to live the rest of my life. Although I had always suffered from low self-esteem, in the back of my mind, I knew I could be doing something more. Suddenly, all of these things started to come together. So in 1968 I went back to graduate school to work toward my Ph.D. in English literature.

"As soon as I enrolled in the Ph.D. program, I began to see my husband in a different light. I had always viewed him as much smarter than me. I had always subordinated my career to his. I put him so many rungs above me that when the idealization fell away, the relationship withered. I no longer made him the center of my universe. Two years into my graduate work, we separated. When I got a doctorate—something he had never achieved—we divorced."

A telling event occurred in Roxanne's life after she separated from her husband. She enrolled in a Jungian training institute and eventually became a Jungian analyst. At an age when most people think about retiring, she began a new professional career and, in her case, it was the same career pursued by her ex-husband.

Roxanne had uncovered a secret that many bright, intelligent women hold: that they choose to emotionally stand behind men who are doing the work that they themselves could do, with the same or even greater degree of skill and success. "All along," Roxanne says, "I wanted to *be* him, but I never quite realized it. And it's a lot more fun and a lot more rewarding to be myself.

"I've been seeing patients in private practice for nine years now. I work about twenty hours a week. I'm just beginning to publish in the professional literature for the first time in my life. It's wonderful."

Roxanne has no regrets that it took her so long to wake up to her own promise. "The most important thing to me is to feel fulfilled and to believe that what I do is important to society. This month a psychotherapy journal will publish a paper of mine. I am very proud of this contribution. For the first time in my life I really feel like I'm exercising my potential. I had to separate from my husband before I could appreciate my own capabilities. I had to learn that women truly are capable and important and that I had it all inside of me. I'm glad I learned it before it was too late."

Women in middle age have a tremendous reserve of resources and energy. Added to their brains and strength are life experience and knowledge of human nature. Yet change is seldom easy. Reconstructing a life always involves a difficult stage when new goals are identified and strategies planned. For the older woman, that stage may also mean rediscovering and activating a forgotten part of herself.

RECAPTURING THE PAST

It had taken Ingrid, class of '53, forty years to arrive at a point where she was willing to examine past choices and admit that she had turned her back on her tremendous intellectual potential. Ingrid's father died when she was a small child, and her mother took in lodgers to make ends meet. To a great extent, Hunter compensated for the drabness of her home environment. "School was a feast for me. I devoured everything I read like a starved child—art, science, history. Literature was my foremost love, and I remember the pure ecstasy of learning to read in different languages and practicing translating back and forth among them just for fun. My mother and our neighbors never understood anything about my school, so I always lived in two separate worlds."

Ingrid was valedictorian of her senior class, and went directly into Hunter College. She graduated in three-and-one-half years, Phi Beta Kappa, *summa cum laude,* and was offered a scholarship to study classics at Oxford.

But Ingrid was in love with a young student from Fordham University. "It's hard to explain now, it was so long ago. I wanted security, I wanted to belong somewhere. I didn't want to go off to England by myself. I decided to stay home and marry Steven. I can remember the look of disappointment in the eyes of my classics professor at Hunter when I turned down the scholarship."

In her other world, however, Ingrid received wholehearted approval for her decision. Even though Steven was Catholic and Ingrid was not, Ingrid's mother felt marriage was a much better choice than leaving home to study mysterious subjects at a "foreign" university. "I got a lot of approval from my mother and our friends for this choice to marry, so it felt good."

Ingrid embraced Steven's family, and converted to Catholicism before they were married. Looking back at it now, Ingrid says she didn't really make a choice, she just went along with what made sense for that time and place. It's hard for a young woman to stand alone. Religion and marriage provided a sense of security and identity for Ingrid. "When I told people 'I'm a Catholic' it was like I suddenly knew who I was. I can't describe what this felt like, but for the first time in my life I had a sense of being like other people."

By draping a ready-made identity around herself, Ingrid fell into a pattern that would make it more difficult, as the years wore on, to get in touch with her inner self.

Within a few years Ingrid and Steven had two children, then in quick succession five more. "I enjoyed being a mother," Ingrid said. "I threw myself passionately into the job. It was the ultimate act of creation—molding lives, seeing them take shape, becoming the mover, the shaker, the matriarch. I was the best wife, the best mother, the best Catholic. For the next twenty-five years, my life was filled every second. There were a few times in between pregnancies when I did some substitutue teaching. Every time I thought about going to work full-time, I got pregnant again."

Ingrid knew that she had powerful intellectual gifts, but told herself that she made good use of them by teaching her own children. "Raising my children to be productive members of society was my primary career. According to today's society, I guess my career would be judged as mediocre; I personally feel that I have added to the world more than I have taken away from it. What more can one ask in the way of success?"

Even so, Ingrid admitted that most of the time she operated on automatic pilot. "Ours was a feel-good family. I loved them and I loved our life together—but, yes, I knew I was a twelve-cylinder engine running on one cylinder.

"The day I found myself teaching one son to drive and another to walk, I sat down with my husband and asked, basically, 'Is this all there is?' He was perplexed and had no idea what my problem was. I didn't either, but I knew that I had missed the boat."

Ingrid began teaching secondary school full-time. "Now, of course, I was a full-time everything—full-time teacher, full-time mother, full-time wife. I was doing the same as always, only more so." Steven, also a high school teacher, was not happy with Ingrid's choice. He felt she was neglecting the children and urged her to stay home more.

"It was a moot point, because as a newcomer to the faculty, I was the first to get cut when we had layoffs. I was still licking my wounds when the roof fell in. Steven had a stroke. I couldn't believe it. He was only in his forties, and we still had five kids at home. I went into the business of nursing him, and also had to get another job. He seemed to be getting stronger, then, quite suddenly, he suffered another stroke and died.

"I get furious thinking about this because I blame him for dying. He lived as if nothing could ever harm him. He indulged himself—he wouldn't quit smoking, he wouldn't eat right, he wouldn't exercise—he wouldn't even play golf. He left me with two teenagers still in high school and three in college. I was fifty-two years old, and I felt like the rest of my life would be just keeping up."

All of her married life, Ingrid had lived with a self that was small and secure, her identity bordered by the expectations of her family and friends. After Steven died, that world shrunk even further, and Ingrid's own sense of mortality began to prey on her mind.

"I was plagued with morbid thoughts, and I couldn't pull myself together. With the family to take care of, I wanted to speed up the mourning process, so I decided to enter group therapy. I thought it would help me get back on my feet faster." In talking about her life to the women in her group, Ingrid explained that she had simply played the hand life dealt her. "I told them that the cards were so stacked, the social pressures so extreme in the 1950s—I just got married and my family became my life. I told them how I felt about losing everything and never having the opportunity to develop my potential."

Ingrid said she expected a wave of sympathy and understanding from the other women in the group. Instead, she received an avalanche of irritation.

"Ingrid, you're a wimp. You didn't have to stay home and wash diapers for twenty years!"

"You didn't have to have so many kids. Catholics do use birth control, you know."

"I'll bet your husband would have waited for you if you had gone to Oxford. If not, his tough luck!"

"All that time, you never went back to school? How could you do that to yourself?"

Ingrid: "I was stunned at their reaction. I felt like I was running a feminist gauntlet."

At the time, Ingrid fled the therapy session, vowing never to return. When she got home she called a friend and vented her rage. She also told her oldest daughter how she had been "humiliated."

She was surprised when both gently suggested that she might think about what the group members had said. After a few days, Ingrid cooled off. Disturbed by the comments of the women who had confronted her, she began to wonder if they hadn't been right.

Ingrid took a hard look at her life. She recognized that she had had opportunities to stretch her potential and that she had deliberately turned her back on them. Before she can move on, the intelligent woman who has pretended to be ordinary, who has lived without challenging or expanding her talents, must come to terms with her own denial. Admitting the pretense is the first step to getting back on track.

"I had ignored that other self inside, telling myself that it wasn't important. It felt horrible to think that I had missed my opportunities and been dishonest with myself, and that no one but me was responsible. About the time I was grappling with this, my first grandchild was born. I began to get into the business of helping my daughter and being 'Grandma' the way I had been 'Mom.' I was turning away from my other self again, but now I could see myself doing it."

Ingrid returned to the group. She talked more about her life, but this time she was the one who was angry. "I was suddenly angry—with my family for demanding so much from me, angry with myself for being sucked into it. I admitted that it was nobody's fault but my own. I was also mad at the group, on general principle, and I told them so. I thought they had a mean attitude.

"I expected them to be all hostile to me again, but instead they egged me on, 'You tell 'em, gal.' I didn't know where I was going with all this, but I was stirred up."

Ingrid had entered the "awareness" phase of Active Engagement, a period in which she became particularly vulnerable to self-blame regarding her "wasted" years. Bright women tend to be perfectionistic, unforgiving of their own mistakes. They have trouble granting themselves the same tolerance that they extend to others. "Once I got started, I took so much responsibility for the past that it turned into a litany of self-blame.

"Before I could move on, I needed to say, 'Yes, I'm responsible for my actions,' but also, I had to make room for the forces of society. The expectations of the time in which I grew up had overpowered me, and in my youth I didn't have enough emotional resources to resist."

On a sweltering morning in July, as Ingrid listlessly scanned *The New York Times*, she saw an article from the State University of New York at Stony Brook offering scholarships for older women returning to school. On impulse, she applied. "As soon as I filled out the application, I felt an emotional lift."

Her family thought she was foolish. "My mother-in-law said, 'Why not relax and enjoy life?' I didn't know how to rationally explain what I was doing, so I closed my ears and just kept on trucking."

In graduate school, Ingrid was both exhilarated and frightened. She was on the brink of bringing out and redefining herself, the inner self she had kept cloaked and hidden for twenty-five years. She felt intimidated by the younger students around her, and they in turn seemed threatened by her all-knowing wisdom. "I had to resist a tendency to mother my classmates," she said. "At the same time, as I sat in the classroom all those years later, I knew I was smarter than anybody there, and always had been."

After one year in graduate school, Ingrid accepted a fellowship in London at a child study center. She stepped back in time and picked up the threads of her youth. "I was lucky that my old dreams were still accessible at my age. I know that isn't always the case, but for me, it was still possible to study, and to begin the work I had put aside all those years ago."

THE RESUMERS

A harsh reality may eventually confront a woman who completely drops out of the work force to raise her family. With obsolete skills and uncertain goals, she may find it very difficult to find a place for herself if she chooses to return to work. This happens frequently when women are forced to suddenly reenter the workplace because of economic necessity. And yet, dozens of older women in our study demonstrated that it was never too late to take risks.

Widowed at age fifty, Janet, class of '42, decided to return to school. "I worried that because I had fewer productive years ahead of me, I wouldn't be a good candidate for graduate school. A friend asked me, 'How old will you be in five years if you go back to school—and how old will you be if you don't?' Not very subtle or profound, but I got the message. I had done years of volunteer work in the community, running every kind of fundraising campaign and charitable organization. I was able to get a scholarship earmarked for 'resumers' to study business administration."

In fact, "resumers" have remarkably successful academic achievements. Statistics show that older women returning to school receive honors at twice the rate of their younger colleagues. Smith College president, Dr. Mary Maples Dunn, quoted in the Special Education Section of the Spring 1988 issue of *The New York Times*, said: "They are a great asset academically, intellectually, and socially. When a woman has waited twenty years to go back to class, she doesn't fool around."

This period of reentry is a prime time for women to set their sights on leadership roles and aim for targets that previously eluded their imagination and vision. The critical issue is not how many years a woman has left, but what she chooses to do with them.

After earning a master's degree Janet got a job in hospital administration. Five years later, she was named director of a large mental health facility in upstate New York. "I'm basically doing what I had done in my volunteer work—running a big organization and a huge staff. Now I get a title, recognition, and a big fat paycheck. Occasionally, I wonder where I might be if I had started earlier—but what's the point? This is now, and it's great."

That desire to take command of their lives often comes to

women in their later years. According to Harvard sociologist David Riesman, "There is a yearning for independence among many people, for working at something that's rewarding to them, and in a setting where they are 'least bossed.' "

Charles Handy, a professor at the London Business School, reminds us that "Ideas do not require too much capital, just imagination, and the energy and ability to make things happen." Handy says that maximum freedom is achieved at the expense of security, what he calls the "ancient trade-off." Some people will always need to have a boss or someone to tell them what to do and how to do it. But smart women in midlife and older often reach a point where they are ready to take the "boss" role for themselves. This happened to one of our Hunter women, who was forced by circumstances into a more rewarding life than she had ever imagined for herself.

GAIL, class of '50: "I never wanted anything more than to take care of my family and live the way my parents did—a successful husband, a nice home, and good kids. I didn't know that my husband was a lousy businessman and that he was getting us further and further into debt with his gambling habit. I had refused to wake up to the truth until we lost everything we had, including our house. I had to get a job, fast. I had never actually worked before and I really didn't have any skills. I couldn't even get a waitressing job, because I had no experience. I finally got a job as a hostess in a restaurant because I had a relative in the business. The first day, I didn't know whether I could last through my shift. The second day, I had the routine down cold. By the end of the week, I could have run the restaurant. It's one tough business, let me tell you. But the truth is, I loved it. It's fast and furious, it's murder having to get along with so many different kinds of people. I worked my way up to manager.

"I wound up owning my own place. I know, it sounds like Mildred Pierce, but it happened to me. I had a talent for managing people, which is ninety percent of a successful business—you have to keep all the wheels spinning."

●

The Hunter women who were in midlife at the time of our study had been raised with traditional expectations, but were also of an age where they had experienced the awakening of the women's movement. We expected to discover that they were capable of change at this stage of their lives. The surprise was that all women—even those who were older and not so directly influenced by the push for women's rights in the 1970s—had demonstrated a similar capacity when they had entered their fifties and sixties. Midlife seems to offer bright women a flight of the mind, and also peak experiences of freedom and creativity.

KITTY, class of '33, the bookkeeper who had left her job with Underwood Typewriter after the end of World War II: "I stayed home for twenty years. All those years I did volunteer work, tutoring and fundraising. I nursed my youngest daughter through childhood arthritis when no one knew anything about it. When we finally got the right diagnosis at Columbia Presbyterian Hospital, the doctor said to me, 'I would be proud if I was the one who encouraged you to enter the field of medicine.' But how could I even consider going to medical school when I had two young children?"

It wasn't until her daughters were in college that Kitty decided to go back to work. She had serious misgivings, unsure that her obsolete skills could win her a desirable job. Like many women in this situation, Kitty needed a support network to refresh her skills and help conquer her fears. For Kitty, help came from an adult education program.

"I took a course called 'The Mature Woman Returns to the Business World.' Then I got an accounting job in which I was responsible for the bookkeeping of federal grant funds for a large nonprofit organization. I only expected to work part-time, but the head of my department retired, and I was the natural successor for the job. I couldn't see it going to anyone else. I'm good at handling people, planning work, allocating work. I'm a good executive. So I took the job. I was never the sort of person who could take great leaps and do anything daring, but I succeeded in every job I took on.

"When I was sixty-five my company gave incentives for early retirement. My boss was surprised when I took it. He said, 'We didn't mean for *you* to take retirement.' "

Even after she left her job, Kitty continued working for her community. "I did tax counseling for the elderly. I also did literacy volunteering. I joined clubs, and became treasurer of the women's guild at our church."

In this stage of her life, Kitty rejects trying to live up to someone else's standards and avoids dwelling on any negative consequences of her choices. "I'm blessed with children who love me and think I'm great. My daughter, the lawyer, said to a friend at work, 'My sister, Jenny, is reliving my mother's life. I'm living out my mother's dream.' She's right. She's living out my dream of the big career, the important career, the career where she gets both recognition and money. It escaped me."

ON THE WINGS OF AGE

The flight of mind doesn't stop at age sixty-five. Edwin Shneidman, a professor at UCLA, says, "It seems likely that being born bright—with good organs including a good brain—adds years to the end of life from the very beginning. In addition, using one's mind and being intellectually busy during one's life may well add an active decade to a life that might ordinarily slow to a near stop around age seventy."

We saw the older Hunter graduates defining their lives for themselves, fulfilling their potential in unique ways. Women often need to take some time to think about who they are, what makes them happy, and what they want from their life.

In our study, the older Hunter women fulfilled the vision of Louis Terman. Terman's study of three hundred gifted students began in 1921; recently, researchers George E. Vaillant and Caroline O. Vaillant studied the women from the original group and found that, despite the limited opportunities for career development, these exceptionally bright women continued to engage in creative pursuits at age seventy-five and beyond.

The Vaillants write in the January 1990 issue of *The American Journal of Psychiatry*: "As we read through their long case records, we watched parents sending their bright daughters out to support the family during the Depression. We watched the separations and divorces associated with World War II make the Terman women into single mothers without alimony. Throughout we watched the socialization of adulthood nip promising careers in the bud. This was painful. In contrast, the late-life flowering of these women was reassuring, and we suspect that retention of the capacity for play may be a critical ingredient for successful aging. Perhaps only adults who have not forgotten how to play are those likely to put something in the world that was not there before."

We saw this same pattern in all of the older Hunter women. Without exception, our graduates over the age of seventy were energetic, humorous, and vividly contemporary. Helen, for the class of 1911, became a lawyer back in the days when women were never lawyers. "I've always achieved any goal I set for myself," she said. "I'm ninety-seven years old. The attendants at my nursing home complain that I do things alone. I say to the other old ladies, 'Never mind the torpedoes—full steam ahead!' " Sylvia, a '50s graduate, who did not complete medical school until she was forty-one, still practices medicine at the age of seventy-nine. "I'm still working because I'm good, because I'm contributing, and because I love it."

Regina, until the day she died at age ninety-three, was still giving talks and writing book reviews for her Connecticut newspaper; Irene, in her eighties, continues to work with dedication for the betterment of her neighborhood; Kitty, in her late seventies, works for her church league, helps older people with their taxes, and teaches adults to read. Roxanne, at age sixty-six, embarked on an entirely new profession as an analyst.

•

Betty Friedan might have been speaking of these women when she recently said, "I predict we're about to see a breakthrough in the area of roles for older people. Just as twenty-five years ago I looked at women and saw problems that had no name, I now look at older people—especially women—and see strengths that have no name."

ELEVEN

ACTIVE

ENGAGEMENT

*Women have to learn how to take risks, defy
conventions, and go against the system.*

—ROXANNE, class of '43

We wanted to define just what we meant by women fulfilling their
potential and achieving success in their lives. We concluded that
all things being equal, success is the integration of all parts of a
woman's life.

Achievement can be at any *self-determined* level—top leadership in business, arts, politics—or top-flight homemaker, teacher,
fundraiser. The woman defines the arena, the level, and the satisfaction of her accomplishments, unwilling to be governed by the
demands or expectations of others.

Throughout their lives, women confront critical choice points
intrinsic to their life stages. Their journeys are like a spiral pathway,
circling, moving forward, sometimes falling back on their own steps
in order to stay on the path.

Smart women today grow up assuming many things—that they
will have unfettered choices, opportunities to work in interesting
jobs, helpful mates, and workplaces with ceilingless domes. They
are surprised when the burden of compromise seeps into their daily
lives. Women mainly remain the ones to alter behavior, even their

personalities, to accommodate others. They are still the ones expected to adapt, cope, and twist themselves into contortions; the ones who pay too big a price for "getting along" and "going along," with no true accommodation from the people and the world around them.

To make critical choices, women must first see their dilemma clearly. We asked Irene, class of '24, "What do you think stops women in this era, when there is so much more opportunity?"

IRENE: "Probably the same thing that has always stopped them. The barriers to the top are less visible, but they're still there. It's hard to know how to get over them."

The reality is that society has not restructured its thinking and actions to meet the aspirations of today's women. In the 1990s, many hurdles still exist. How can women fulfill their potential and gain the support and courage to leap over them and reach the top? We believe that by recognizing critical choice points, and acting on them, women can begin to extricate themselves from traditional restrictions. It requires a hard look at the reality that surrounds them, as well as listening to their own inner voices.

Many intelligent women feel uncomfortable when they slow down to reflect on their lives and careers. Looking backward, they can see critical choice points bypassed in the past still faintly illuminated. The future stretches before them. Risking change now is scary. The gains could be far-reaching—jobs with more satisfaction, more money; respect; pride in their own integrity; new relationships. But it's a given that you cannot embrace the new without first letting go of the old. How do you know if change is worth the risk? Or what price you will have to pay?

Active Engagement carries with it the potential for both positive and negative consequences. Women who choose Active Engagement feel the danger inherent in the act. Asserting personal freedom almost always generates opposition.

It is diminishing to say that any capable woman can achieve her goals even when they have been shoved aside, sidetracked, and placed in the unclaimed freight yard. A woman with few resources at her disposal will have a hard time making a place for herself. The vast majority of women in our study were well educated and all were extremely intelligent. We saw that even for them establishing and attaining certain goals often seemed impossible.

In their pattern of living up to expectations, they swung between two points—at the turn of this century, choice was not much of a problem because there were few choices to be made. Now, approaching the next century, young women tell us they have so many options they cannot make a decision. In both extremes we see a common factor: women throughout the century were seldom prepared in childhood and encouraged throughout adult life to make independent choices.

WHAT MAKES THE DIFFERENCE?

Psychologist Judith Bardwick of the University of Michigan writes in *In Transition*: "The crucial question has changed. It is no longer, Are you employed? It is, How ambitious are you?"

It has been said that an individual's GQ—gumption quotient—is a more reliable indicator of ability and future success than her IQ.

This is also the conclusion found in Professor Lewis Terman's monumental study of three hundred intellectually gifted students whose careers were followed long after they graduated from high school.

Terman described four traits that marked gifted students who later went on to achieve goals commensurate with their abilities: persistence; self-confidence; lives well integrated with their professional goals; and freedom from feelings of inferiority.

Professor Terman concluded: "In the total picture the greatest contrast between the two groups was in all-round emotional and social adjustment and in drive to achieve."

The drive to achieve, Terman said, explained in large measure the success of some bright people and the relative failure of others.

But his explanation raises a question which has never been adequately answered. Where does "drive" come from?

Some studies have shown that family plays a pivotal role; others point to social and economic status (women from poorer families with immigrant parents have been shown to be more ambitious). The studies have been few and small, and we don't know if their findings are valid.

Our own study was similarly inconclusive. We found that, even without family nurturing and encouragement, some women advanced anyway. Some others who were carefully nurtured still were unable to advance. While no single factor predicted either result, significant clues appeared consistently that seemed to exert a negative or slowing effect on the "excellence factor."

In youth:

- Being perfect little girls
- Lack of counseling and guidance
- Few nontraditional role models.

In adult life:

- Lack of networking and mentoring in the workplace
- Isolation and discrimination on the job
- Juggling family responsibilities and career with little assistance from spouse or employers.

In addition, certain emotional components colored every facet of their lives:

- An unwillingness to admit and be proud of being smart
- A fear of taking risks
- An inability to see—and take responsibility for—their choices.

Although the repercussions are not recognized until adult life, roots of the missing courage factor must lie in a woman's childhood, the greenhouse in which the seedpods of leadership form and begin to grow.

Although many of the Hunter women had stable, loving parents, usually their parents articulated only the vaguest career goals for their daughters. As little girls they had rapidly grasped how society frowns upon anger in women, ridicules independent thinking, rejects bold and controversial actions. Even very young females are smart enough to know that severe consequences can follow if they deviate from what is expected.

Young females need help to recognize their own talents and abilities. They need someone to help them set challenging goals. Someone who encourages them to take risks; to begin, even as children, to aim high, strive for honors and awards, and learn the skills of leadership.

ROXANNE, class of '43, said: "The truth is, men learn how to assume leadership by fitting in with the status quo; women have to do just the opposite—they have to learn how to take risks, defy conventions, and go against the system. I think to do this you need special preparation when you're young."

Those smart girls who escape, or overcome, the tyranny of perfection seem more willing to take risks as adults and thus put themselves in the position to achieve leadership.

Children who go their own way may appear on the surface to be extremely selfish. They may turn inward and become secretive, trying to hibernate until childhood has run its course. They are sometimes angry and rebellious.

HELENE, class of '62, is a woman who deviated markedly from her family's expectations from the time she insisted on enrolling at Hunter, deciding to become a city planner, marrying "outside" her family's tightly knit structure, and later divorcing her husband. She was able to trust a voice within herself, and started to go against her family when she was only eleven years old. Such women often describe themselves as self-made and report feeling different from their families at an early age. "I see myself as a woman who has shaped her own life. My family's expectations were different from how I turned out. But I feel good about where I've ended up, and how, many years later, I've been able to fit into my family, and gain their love and respect on my own terms."

Helene was the exception. We found that most female children mold themselves to parental expectations. Because a girl's emotional development is largely set before she reaches school, it's up to parents to encourage and prepare a daughter for leadership. Parents can help a daughter identify her own goals and learn to make her own choices. They can provide encouragement and support that will help her withstand the inevitable setbacks that accompany ambition. When she falls short of "perfection" or makes mistakes, parents can give her the confidence to accept failure and move forward. Parents can also discuss conflicts their daughter feels about achievement versus social acceptance, about how to make choices for herself, about the price she may have to pay if she chooses to pursue an unconventional path.

For parents, the critical ingredient in bringing up daughters who grow into confident and risk-taking adults is to demonstrate these same attitudes and behaviors in the family, since a child learns from the example of her parents and other adults.

We also saw how women in adolescence were already in the habit of steering clear of choice points and avoiding risks. Almost all of the Hunter graduates said that as young students they had admired and respected their teachers, and almost in the same breath, said they received virtually no counseling or encouragement to develop leadership roles.

This huge void in the midst of their elementary and secondary school years would never be breached by most. It was not filled in college, and certainly remained empty in the workplace. They needed guidance to help them imagine future creative lives, clear-sighted information to observe barriers that stood in their way and devise strategies to overcome them. Little of this was present in the lives of the Hunter women. Seldom did they aspire to the top or dream of leadership.

•

The Hunter women told us how difficult change can be. They remembered the critical choice points in their lives, how frequently they were turned away from challenges by prevailing social forces.

Young women of today still have the advantage of youth to boost themselves into leadership ranks. They have the added benefit of growing up in a time when society has opened new pathways for women. They may be the women best able to make their own choices. That they still must struggle to do so comes as a surprise to many of them. Several of our youngest women told us that amid seemingly myriad options, finding a goal is elusive. Because they had never been brought up to choose independently, they are suddenly plunged into adult life without the necessary equipment to meet their critical choice points.

Joyce and Toni fit the description of the contemporary young women who seem to have everything, but in fact whose security and sense of worth have been eroded by the treacherous currents of modern life. Living in a decade of increased opportunities for women, they seem to face even more pressures than their predecessors.

Joyce, for example, our overprotected, talented 1982 graduate, has both the brains and the education to achieve much of what she desires. She has had a loving mother who supported and nourished her every step of the way. But Joyce faces two tremendous challenges which could keep her from fulfilling her potential. She is black, which she knows is a disadvantage in many situations. And she has been, by her own description, overprotected, which has left her feeling dependent and somewhat incompetent.

She is swamped by the possibilities that exist for her, but desperately wishes someone else would supply a formula for decision-making. But there is no magic formula. Everyone struggles to make choices. It is the struggle that's important.

Before choices can be made, a woman first may have to recapture her inner self. For young women this usually involves identifying the limiting factors of their childhood that held them back;

separating from their parents and becoming responsible individuals; strengthening the true self by developing their own values. These three tasks are all interconnected and are usually accomplished together.

A young woman on the brink of a crucial choice in her life must ask herself:

If I were certain of success, what would my dream be? What would I dare to aim for?

The second question is, Am I brave enough to try it, even though there are no guarantees and I may fail?

Once a woman identifies and accepts her vision as well as her anxieties, she can gain confidence and courage to become the hero in a life of challenges, adventure, and fulfillment.

For women further along in their life stages, the question asked by the philosopher Martin Buber seems like a clarion call: "If not now, when?" Some women have gone through life with the true self so hidden that they have lost touch with their own values and desires. As adults they may suffer severe depression and isolation, a floating discontent. Something is trying to come to the surface.

Moments of crisis erupt as the pressure builds up inside. Each crisis is a challenge to act. If a woman fails to act, the crisis eventually subsides and her life resumes, apparently unchanged. A small psychic scar marks her refusal to engage. Periods of crisis continue to randomly erupt. In the end, she is left with a pervasive sense of hopelessness and helplessness.

A woman who recognizes in herself the pleasing female bending her will for others can still make a choice for herself. There is no timetable for a woman to choose risk rather than security. The status quo can be overthrown at any time in her development, although time often makes risk seem more expensive.

What gets women going again? Sometimes a chance encounter with an old friend, sometimes seeing a child leave home and begin to accomplish what Mother has always wanted to do. Sometimes a fierce argument with a husband. Sometimes merely the realization that life doesn't go on forever and it's now or never.

A turning point arrives when a woman recognizes that until now she has hidden a part of herself, that she is governed by how she *should* behave, how she *should* react, and how she *should* feel in any given situation. She begins to question: What would have happened if she had, even as a child, shown her real feelings? She is exhausted and sick and tired of the way things are. Now she is ready to make a move.

What is particularly fulfilling to a woman at midlife or as a resumer making critical choices are the new challenges and the satisfaction reaped in meeting them. By exploring new pathways—frightening as they may be—and feeling the excitement of new possibilities, a woman in midlife can enjoy a new level of life without the inner and external barriers that once confined and restricted her.

BLUEPRINT FOR CHANGE

Active Engagement is a process by which women face their situation and their choices squarely; reflect on the significance of those choices; accept responsibility for them; and risk acting on their decisions.

Active Engagement says that we all have a choice, and our choices are valid as long as we make them out of our own consciousness and exercise of free will. We can choose to maintain the status quo or to be creative and experiment.

Change can occur at any point at which a woman begins to see that she has a choice. Often, an overwhelming feeling of dissatisfaction is the prime motivator.

Her intentions may simmer for a long time before she takes action. Or change may be quick: when an individual is ready to change, it may not take long to do it. Encouragement—or discouragement—from others is a powerful factor that can propel or impede action.

Change takes effort and stamina and, most of all, guts. If a woman is to take advantage of her opportunities, she must thread into the fabric of her self-image feelings of control and power, and fearlessness. Even though the fear will be there, the desire to master it will be stronger.

A drama takes place in the life of a woman who dares embark on such a venture. Creating a life that is realistic, fulfilling, and worthy of her gifts means actively engaging all of the obstacles that hold her back—those in the world and those inside of herself. Four steps are common to Active Engagement:

1. *Awareness of Critical Choice Points.* The first important step in the process of Active Engagement is the recognition of a critical choice point and the similar recognition that a response is required. Some Hunter women had seen the critical choice points in their lives, but turned their backs on them. Some had not seen them at all. Many "stumbled" across their choice points, and attributed their decisions to circumstance: "I did it because I had to . . . because my mother made me . . . because that's the way things were."

2. *Reflection.* A period of reflection precedes every important decision. This time is often rich in memory as women recall important people in their lives, particularly their mothers, grandmothers, and teachers, and begin to see their influences. Reflection may also be accompanied by feelings of emotional discomfort and restlessness.

Sometimes it feels like floundering. Yet struggling with ideas and weighing the possibilities are a necessary part of the process and essential to change. A woman's roles are often fluid and contiguous, and her priorities one day need not be the same on another. During this phase it's good to remember that choosing to explore one avenue doesn't mean you have to live on that street for the rest of your life.

3. *Taking Responsibility.* Taking responsibility for choices is different from blaming yourself if you fail. Self-blame leads to sorrow and depression. Taking responsibility, on the other hand, leads to growth. Facing the truth squarely leads to greater control and maturity. If the outcome of a choice proves to be less than you desired,

you are ready to move on to the next challenge. If it works, and if you are flying on the wings of success, you can—and should—take the credit.

4. *Taking Action.* Risk is a powerful component of Active Engagement. You cannot fulfill the ultimate freedom of choice until you are willing to act, and action always means risk. The risk may be large or small, it may be financial or personal or political, or all three. You cannot fulfill your potential without it.

There is a big gap between awareness and taking action. The process of breaking through, in which many cherished beliefs and old ways of rationalizing are shattered, is essential for change. It may temporarily leave one feeling frightened and disorganized. Then comes that moment when something clicks, and you can do it.

Inevitably, there will be someone—usually someone you care deeply about—that you have to cross. You will have to risk that person's displeasure, perhaps rejection, when you make your move. But not to do so would mean losing too much self-esteem in your own eyes. Grace faced and tolerated the rage of her boss when she quit her job; Roxanne put her marriage on the line and was rejected by her husband when she pursued her own career; Phyllis must still face a showdown with her mother and her husband. The person we are so anxious about confronting is always that individual who wields the most psychological control over us. To face that person down and stand up for your own rights requires a true act of bravery. It is hard to do, but you will feel powerful afterward.

• TWELVE •

CONCLUSION

Every woman who has ever had a plan or a dream can find the courage to make a personal commitment to fulfill her promise. Women who become actively engaged in the creation of their own lives will find that others will eagerly follow them.

Contemporary women have learned to swing and sway with the changing times. An increasing number of today's adolescents and young women have mothers who are doctors, lawyers, and top executives. Their mothers have overcome obstacles and achieved success. The daughters now, stepping along the same spiraling lanes, will have to make further innovative decisions.

Pulitzer Prize–winning playwright Wendy Wasserstein has said that what is missing in "making a better world" is the "we" component. Wasserstein believes that it is essential for women not only to fulfill their own potential, but to ensure that others can pursue theirs, too. The ideas that capture us and make women want to construct a better society have to be there to hold on to.

Many of our graduates expressed a similar philosophy, that

women in their run for the top have to hold on to the best part of themselves, the part that is viewed as uniquely female.

IRENE, class of '24: "If women act like men they may eventually break through to the top by copying the prevailing attitude—more money, more power. In my opinion, if women get on top like a man, they will make very little difference in the world. What we need are more articulate leaders who have good values in life, caring, life-preserving. Leaders who first have those ideals, and then have the power to express them in a way that will enlarge the lives of everyone. That's what I'd like to see women leaders do, if they can."

Whether they seek careers, head for the heights, adopt the male model of success or totally reject it, juggle jobs and motherhood—whatever their choices—women are aware that their decisions do not come easy.

KITTY, class of '33, pointed out that there is always a trade-off: "Everybody has to do it her own way. You can choose anything you want to do, if you are willing to pay the price."

When we began the interviews we had an uneasy feeling that many of the younger graduates had no interest in picking up the torch for women's advancement. We were gratified to learn that in large part we were mistaken. Many of the younger women said they felt challenged by their interviews with us, and a few later reported back that they had "got to thinking" about these issues. They weren't certain how they would proceed, but said they had made a decision to try.

Contemporary women may be less caught up in trying to act like Wonder Woman. They are more willing to admit that to soar to the top they need a change in the system. They needn't feel they are letting the side down if they admit it. Ten years ago there was a genuine fear in the workplace that if women admitted how difficult it was to do everything, they would be shown the door. There has been a real "If you can't stand the heat . . ." mentality on the job.

Slowly, however, young women are beginning to voice their

dissatisfaction. Why shouldn't the system change? What's so impossible about child care, leaves of absence, pay equity?

Dr. Iolanda E. Low, a professor at Harvard Medical School, says, "There can be no doubt today that many women all over this country (some even opposed to female liberation) want to reexamine themselves as human beings, asking 'Who am I? Can I be more?' and searching for broader horizons and clearer directions for their own and their children's lives."

Young women today can look at the generation of women just preceding them and observe how they used their imaginations, their skills, and their intelligence to crystallize their own visions. They have before them role models who confronted problems, worked out strategies, and acted on them—women who took responsibility for the consequences of their choice. These successful women inspire younger women to do the same, to believe that they can control their surroundings and effect change. Older women need to help them, remind them, encourage them to tolerate and survive adversity and continue to move onward.

Some women in our study, many of whom have been honored in the Hunter Hall of Fame, made choices that enabled them to achieve high levels in unexpected fields, despite the problems inherent in politics and power. Women like Metropolitan Opera star Martina Arroyo, class of '53; author and teacher Hortense Calisher, class of '28; Constance Eberhart Cook, class of '38, the New York State legislator who led the successful fight for abortion reform in 1970; Shirley Schlanger Abrahamson, class of '50, who became the first woman justice of the Wisconsin Supreme Court; union leader Belle Zeller, class of '21; writer and scholar Cynthia Ozick, class of '46; Minna Speigel Rees, first woman president of the American Association for the Advancement of Science, and president of CUNY Graduate Division; and Dr. Bernadine Healy, class of '62, Director of National Institutes of Health.

They pulled hard against the grain; their accomplishments brilliant, their numbers few. They had the ability to cope with failure and frustration, and believed they could succeed. They attributed their accomplishments to luck, courage, perseverance, and changes in society that opened new opportunities.

We wish similar success for every woman—success measured by the involvement of her whole being in the exploration of her diverse talents, success characterized by the flowering of her intelligence—and most importantly—the fulfillment of her dreams.

BIBLIOGRAPHY

Anastasi, A. 1982. *Psychological testing*. 5th ed. New York: Macmillan.

Bardwick, J. M. 1976. *In transition: How feminism, sexual liberation, and the search for self-fulfillment have altered America*. New York: Holt, Rienhart & Winston.

Belenky, M. F., et al., 1986. *Women's ways of knowing*. New York: Basic Books.

Bell, L. A. 1989. Something's wrong here and it's not me: Challenging the dilemmas that block girls' success. *Journal for the Education of the Gifted* 123 (2): 118–30.

Belkin, G. S. 1987. *Contemporary psychotherapies*. 2nd ed. Monterey, CA: Brooks/Cole.

Blaubergs, M. S. 1980. The gifted female: Sex-role stereotyping and gifted girls' experience and education. *Roeper Review* 2 (3): 13–20.

Brooks-Gunn, J., and Furstenberg, F. F. 1989. Adolescent sexual behavior. *American Psychologist* 44: 249–57.

Brown, D., et al., eds. 1984. *Career choice and development*. San Francisco: Jossey-Bass.

Bugental, J. F. T. 1967. *Challenges of humanistic psychology*. New York: McGraw-Hill.

Buhler, C. 1935. The curve of life as studied in biographies. *Journal of Applied Psychology* 19: 405–9.

Callahan, C. M. 1979. The gifted and talented women. In *The gifted and talented*, ed. A. H. Pazssow, 401–23. Chicago: National Society for the Study of Education.

Carkhuff, R. R., and Berenson, B. G. 1977. *Beyond counseling and therapy*. 2nd ed. New York: Holt, Rienhart & Winston.

Chusid, H., and Cochran, L. 1989. Meaning of career change from the perspective of family roles and dramas. *Journal of Counseling Psychology* 36: 34–41.

Clance, P. R., and Imes, S. A. 1978. The impostor phenomenon in high-achieving women: Dynamics and therapeutic intervention. *Psychotherapy: Theory, Research and Practice* 15: 241–45.

Colarusso, C. A., and Nemiroff, R. A. 1981. *Adult development*. New York: Plenum Press.

Cole, J. R. and Zuckerman, H. 1987. Marriage, motherhood, and research performance in science. *Scientific American* 256 (2): 119–25.

Collier, H. 1982. *Counseling women: A guide for therapists*. New York: Free Press.

Connelly, F. M., and Clandinin, D. J. 1990. Stories of experience and narrative inquiry. *Educational Researcher* 19 (5): 2–14.

Corsini, R. J., and Wedding, D. 1989. *Current psychotherapies.* Itasca, Il: F. E. Peacock.

Darmofall, S., and McCarbery, R. 1979. Achievement orientation in females: A social psychological perspective. *The Psychological Record* 29: 15–41.

De Beauvoir, S. 1953. *The second sex.* New York: Bantam Books.

Denmark, F. L. 1980. Psyche: From rocking the cradle to rocking the boat. *American Psychologist* 35: 1057–65.

Douvan. E. 1976. The role of models in women's professional development. *Psychology of Women Quarterly* 1 (1): 5–20.

Dunbar, C., et al., 1979. Successful coping styles in professional women. *Canadian Journal of Psychiatry* 24: 43–46.

Eccles, J. S. 1987. Gender roles and women's achievement-related decisions. *Psychology of Women Quarterly* 11: 135–72.

Eichorn, D., et al., eds. 1981. *Present and past in midlife.* New York: Academic Press.

Elder, G. H. 1974. *Children of the great depression: Social change in life experience.* Chicago: University of Chicago Press.

Erikson, E. 1963. *Childhood and society.* New York: W. W. Norton.

The Feminist Majority Report. 1989. The glass ceiling: How women are blocked from getting to the top in business 2 (2 October): 4–5.

Fierman, J. 1990, July 30. Why women still don't hit the top. *Fortune,* Cover story, Managing, 40–62.

Fox, L. H., and Richmond, L. J. 1979: Gifted females: Are we meeting their counseling needs? *Personnel and Guidance Journal* 67: 256–60.

Fox., L. H., et al. 1981. Career development of gifted and talented women. *Journal of Career Education* (June): 289–98.

Fox, L. H., and Zimmerman, W. 1985. Gifted women. In *The Psychology of gifted children*, ed. J. Freeman. New York: John Wiley & Sons.

Friday, N. 1977. *My mother, myself: The daughter's search for identity.* New York: Delacorte Press.

Garrison, V. S., et al., 1986. Are gifted girls encouraged to achieve their occupational potential? *Roeper Review* 9 (2): 101–4.

Gerson, K. 1985. *Hard choices: How women decide about work, career and motherhood.* Berkeley: University of California Press.

Geile, J. Z., ed. 1982. *Women in the middle years: Current knowledge and directions for research and policy.* New York: John Wiley & Sons.

Gilligan, C. 1982. *In a different voice: Psychological theory and women's development.* Cambridge: Harvard University Press.

Gilligan, C., ed. 1990. *Making connections: The relational worlds of adolescent girls at Emma Willard school.* Cambridge: Harvard University Press.

Goldman, L., 1978. ed. *Research methods for counselors: Practical approaches in field settings.* New York: John Wiley & Sons.

Goldman, L. 1971. *Using tests in counseling.* 2nd ed. New York: Appleton-Century-Crofts.

Gould, R. 1978. *Transformations, growth and change in adult life.* New York: Simon and Schuster.

Grau, P. N. 1985. Counseling the gifted girl. *Gifted Child Today* 38: 8–11.

Gunter, N. C., and Gunter, B. G. 1990. Domestic division of labor among working couples. *Psychology of Women Quarterly* 14: 355 –70.

Haensly, P. A. 1990. Protégés, mentorship savvy, and a qualitatively differentiated mentoring process. *Communicator* 20 (1 January): 1–16.

Hall, C., and Lindzey, G. 1978. *Theories of personality.* 3rd ed. New York: John Wiley & Sons.

Heilbrun, C. 1979. *Reinventing womanhood.* New York: W. W. Norton.

Heilbrun, C. 1988. *Writing a woman's life.* New York: Ballantine Books.

Hetherington, E. M, et al., 1989. Marital transitions: A child's perspective. *American Psychologist* 44: 303–12.

Higham, S., and Navarre, J. 1984. Gifted adolescent females require differential treatment. *Journal for Education of the Gifted* 8 (1): 43–58.

Hillman, J. 1975. *Visionary psychology.* New York: Harper & Row.

Hoffman, L. 1972. Early childhood experiences of women's achievement motive. *Journal of Social Issues* 28: 129–55.

Hoffman, L. W. 1989. Effects of maternal employment in the two-parent family. *American Psychologist* 44: 283–92.

Hollinger, C. L., and Fleming, E. S. 1988. Gifted and talented young women: Antecedents and correlates of life satisfaction. *Gifted Child Quarterly* 32 (2): 254–60.

Hollinger, C. L., and Fleming, E. S. 1984. Internal barriers to the realization of potential: Correlates and interrelationships among gifted and talented female adolescents. *Gifted Child Quarterly* 28 (3): 135–39.

Homan, K. B. 1986. Vocation as the quest for authentic existence. *The Career Development Quarterly* (September): 14–23.

Horner, M. 1972. Toward an understanding of achievement-related conflicts in women. *Journal of Social Issues* 28: 157–76.

Horney, K. 1934. *Feminine psychology*. New York: W. W. Norton.

Horney, K. 1937. *The neurotic personality of our time*. New York: W. W. Norton & Co.

Horowitz, F. D., and O'Brien, M. 1986. Gifted and talented children: State of knowledge and directions for research. *American Psychologist* 41: 1147–52.

Horowitz, F. D., and O'Brien, M., eds. 1985. *The gifted and talented: Development perspectives*. Washington, D.C.: The American Psychological Association.

Howard, G. S. 1991. Culture tales: A narrative approach to thinking, cross-cultural psychology, and psychotherapy. *American Psychologist* 46: 187–97.

Howe, M. 1982. Biographical evidence and the development of outstanding individuals. *American Psychologist* 37: 1071–81.

Hurley, D. 1988. The mentor mystique. *Psychology Today*, May, 36–43.

Ivey, A. 1991. *Developmental strategies for helpers: Individual, family and network interventions*. Pacific Grove, CA: Brooks/Cole.

Janeway, E. 1982. *Cross sections: From a decade of change*. New York: William Morrow.

Johnson, P. 1976. Women and power: Toward a theory of effectiveness. *Journal of Social Issues* 32 (3): 99–110.

Kahn, A. 1984. The power war: Male response to power loss under equality. *Psychology of Women Quarterly* 8 (3): 234–47.

Kasworm, C. E. 1990. Adult undergraduates in higher education: A review of past research perspectives. *Review of Educational Research* 60: 345–72.

Kaufman, F. A., et al., 1986. The nature, role and influence of mentors in the lives of gifted adults. *Journal of Counseling and Development* 64: 576–78.

Keller, E. F. 1985. *Reflections on gender and science*. New Haven: Yale University Press.

Kerr, B. 1985. *Smart girls, gifted women*. Columbus: Ohio Psychology Publishing Co.

Kisner, K. 1990. Sowing the seeds of self-doubt: New findings about girls and what women teach them. *Teacher Magazine*, August, 20–21.

Komarovsky, M. 1985. *Women in college: Shaping new feminine identities*. New York: Basic Books.

Kundsin, R. B., ed. 1973. *Successful women in the sciences: An analysis of determinants*. New York: Annals of the New York Academy of Sciences, Vol. 208.

Labich, K. 1991. Can your career hurt your kids? *Fortune*, May 20, 38–68.

Larwood, L., and Gutek, B. A. 1989. *Women's career development*. Newbury Park, CA: Sage Publications.

Lenz, E., and Myerhoff, B. 1985. *The feminization of America: How women's values are changing our public and private lives*. Los Angeles: Jeremy P. Tarcher.

Levinson, D., et al. 1978. *The seasons of a man's life*. New York: Alfred A. Knopf.

Lohman, D. F. 1989. Human intelligence: An introduction to advances in theory and research. *Review of Educational Research* 59 (4): 333–73.

Lopata, H. 1979. The effect of schooling on social contact of urban women. *American Journal of Sociology* 79: 604–19.

Matthews, K. A., and Rodin, J. 1989. Women's changing work roles: Impact on health, family, and public policy. *American Psychologist* 44: 1389–93.

McAdams, D. 1985. *Power, intimacy, and the life story*. Homewood, Il: The Dorsey Press.

McBride, A. B. 1990. Mental health effects of women's multiple roles. *American Psychologist* 45: 381–84.

McKeon, R., ed. 1941. *The basic works of Aristotle*. New York: Random House.

Medmick, M. 1989. On the politics of psychological constructs: Stop the bandwagon, I want to get off. *American Psychologist* 44: 1118–23.

Miller, A. 1981. *Prisoners of childhood: The drama of the gifted child and the search for the true self*. New York: Basic Books.

Miller, B. S. L. and Price, M., eds. 1981. *The gifted child, the family, and the community*. New York: Walker & Co.

Minuchin, S. 1974. *Families and family therapy*. Cambridge: Harvard University Press.

Morrison, A. M., et al., 1987. Executive women: Substance plus style. *Psychology Today.* August, 18–26.

Morrison, A. M., and von Glinow, M. A. 1990. Women and minorities in management. *American Psychologist* 45: 200–8.

Moustakas, C. E. 1967. *Creativity and conformity.* Princeton, N J: D. Van Nostrand Co.

Nadelson, C. C. 1987. Women in leadership roles: Development and challenges. *Adolescent Psychiatry.* 14: 28–41.

Noble, K. 1987. The dilemma of the gifted woman. *Psychology of Women Quarterly* 11: 367–78.

Noble, K. D. 1989. Counseling gifted women: Becoming the heroes of our own stories. *Journal for the Education of the Gifted* 12 (2): 131–41.

Norman, M. 1983. *'Night, mother.* New York: Hill & Wang.

Nozick, R. 1989. *The examined life: Philosophical meditations.* New York: Simon and Schuster.

Olsen, T. 1978. *Silences.* New York: Delacorte Press.

Palmer, S., and Cochran, L. 1988. Parents as agents of career development. *Journal of Counseling Psychology* 35: 71–76.

Patterson, Y. A. 1986. Simone de Beauvoir and the demystification of motherhood. *Yale French Studies* 72: 87–105.

Phillips, S. D., and Bruch, M. A. 1988. Shyness and dysfunction in career development. *Journal of Counseling Psychology* 35 (2): 159–65.

Polkinghorne, D. P. 1988. *Narrative psychology.* Albany, NY: State University of New York Press.

Pollitt, K. 1986. Being wedded is not always bliss. *The Nation,* September 20, 239–42.

Post, R. 1982. Dependency conflicts in high-achieving women: Toward an integration. *Psychotherapy: Theory, Research and Practice* 19: 82–87.

Psychology of Women Quarterly. 1989. 13 (2). Port Chester, NY: Cambridge University Press.

Pyschology of Women Quarterly. 1990. Special Issue: Women at midlife and beyond. 14 (4). Port Chester, NY: Cambridge University Press.

Reger, S., and Galligan, P. 1980. Women in management: An exploration of competing paradigms. *American Psychologist* 35: 902–10.

Reis, S. M. 1987. We can't change what we don't recognize: Understanding the special needs of gifted females. *Gifted Child Quarterly* 31 (2): 83–88.

Reis, S. M., and Callahan, C. M. 1989. Gifted females: They've come a long way—or have they? *Journal for the Education of the Gifted* 12 (2): 99–117.

Rich, S. L., and Phillips, A., eds. 1985. *Women's experience and education.* Cambridge: Harvard Educational Review, Reprint Series No. 17.

Roberts, J. I. 1985. Changing roles of women: Birth of a new reality. *Women and Therapy* 4 (1): 41–51.

Robison-Awana, P., et al., 1986. But what about smart girls? Adolescent self-esteem and sex role perceptions as a function of academic achievement. *Journal of Educational Psychology* 78 (3): 179–83.

Roeper, A. 1978. The young gifted girl: A contemporary view. *Roeper Review* 1 (1): 6–8.

Rogers, C. 1961. *On becoming a person*. Boston: Houghton Mifflin Co.

Saltzman, A. 1991. The executive suite: Why women can't, won't, don't want to, make it to the top. *U.S. News & World Report*, June 17, Cover Story, Business, 38–48.

Scarf, M. 1980. *Unfinished business: Pressure points in the lives of women*. New York: Doubleday.

Schwartz, L. L. 1980. Advocacy for the neglected gifted: Females. *Gifted Child Quarterly* 24 (3): 113–17.

Searle, J. 1984. *Minds, brains and science*. Cambridge: Harvard University Press.

Shaw, C. R. 1966. *The psychiatric disorders of childhood*. New York: Appleton-Century-Crofts.

Sheehy, G. 1976. *Passages: Predictable crises of adult life*. New York: E. P. Dutton.

Shneidman, E. 1989. The Indian summer of life: A preliminary study of septuagenarians. *The American Psychologist* 44: 684–94.

Shweder, R. S., and LeVine, R. A., eds. 1984. *Culture theory: Essays in mind, theory and emotion*. Cambridge, England: Cambridge University Press.

Slavin, R. E. 1990. Achievement effects of ability grouping in secondary schools: A best-evidence synthesis. *Review of Educational Research* 60: 471–500.

Spanard, J-M. A. 1990. Beyond intent: Reentering college to complete the degree. *Review of Educational Research* 60: 309–44.

Steinem, G. 1983. *Outrageous acts and everyday rebellions*. New York: Holt, Rienhart & Winston.

Stone, N. 1989. Mother's work. *Harvard Business Review* 5: 4–8.

Subotnik, R. F., et al., 1989. High IQ children at midlife. An investigation into the generalizability of Terman's genetic studies of genius. *Roeper Review* 11 (3): 139–44.

Terman, L. M. 1925. Mental and physical traits of a thousand gifted children. In *Genetic studies of genius*, L. Terman, ed. Vol 1. Stanford, CA: Stanford University Press.

Terman, L. M., and Oden, M. H. 1947. *Genetic studies of genius*. Vol. 4, *The gifted child grows up*. Stanford, CA: Stanford University Press.

Terman, L. M., and Oden, M. H. 1959. *Genetic studies of genius*. Vol. 5, *The gifted group at mid-life*. Stanford, CA: Stanford University Press.

Unger, R. K. 1984. Hidden assumptions in theory and research on women. In *Women therapists working with women, ed.* C. Brody. New York: Springer Publishing Co.

Vaillant. G. 1977. *Adaptation to life: How the best and brightest came of age*. New York: Little, Brown.

Walker, B. A., and Freeland, T. 1986. Gifted girls grow up. *Journal of the National Association of Women Deans, Administrators and Counselors* 50 (1): 26–32.

Wallis, C. 1989. Onward, women! *Time*, December 4, Cover story: 80–89.

Walsh, M. R. ed. 1987 *The psychology of women: Ongoing debates*. New Haven: Yale University Press.

Webb, J. T., et al., 1983. *Guiding the gifted child: A practical source for parents and teachers*. Columbus: Ohio Psychology Publishing Co.

Weinberg, R. A. 1989. Intelligence and IQ: Landmark issues and great debates. *American Psychologist* 44: 98–104.

Westervelt, E. 1973. Major contributions, a tide in the affairs of women: The psychological impact of feminism on educated women. *The Counseling Psychologist* 4: 3–26.

What's What. 1990, February 28. The Official Newspaper of Hunter College High School: 115 (6): 1–16.

Wheelis, A. 1973. *How people change.* New York: Harper & Row.

Women & Therapy. 1988. 8 (1/2). New York: The Haworth Press.

Yoder, J. D., et al., 1985. To teach is to learn: Overcoming tokenism with mentors. *Psychology of Women Quarterly*: 119–31.

INDEX

A

Abilities, concealing, 58–59
Abrahamson, Shirley Schlanger, 181
Accomplished women, dating and, 128
Achievement
  commensurate with abilities, 170
  factors inhibiting, 123
  and social acceptance, 173
  steady rise in women's, 39–41
Active engagement, 48–50, 168–178
  "awareness" phase of, 160
  four steps common to, 177–78
  process of defined, 49–50
Admission rules, 25
Adolescence, 59

Age 12–13, and critical choice points, 43
Alcohol dependency, 90
All-girl school, advantages of, 83
All-women college, advantages of, 84
American Journal of Psychiatry, The, 166
Anna, Bertha, 18, 20
Anxieties, modern, 147–51
Arroyo, Martina, 181

B

Bardwick, Judith, 170
Barnard College, 104
Binet, Alfred, 25
"Book learning," 28
Buber, Martin, 175

C

Caldicott, Helen, 17
Calisher, Hortense, 181
Callahan, C. M., 24
Career
  changes, 44–45, 152–67
  explorations, 102
  and family relationships, 140–
    143
  finding by accident, 110
  goals, 172
  help in achieving, 42
  nontraditional, 98
Challenges, new, 176
Change
  blueprint for, 176–78
  and recognition of choice, 176
Childless women, negative atti-
    tudes toward, 138
Children of the Great Depression,
    30
Choice, 176
  preparing for independent, 170
College and career guidance, 90–
    94
Common sense, 27, 28
Competition, 84
  and cliques, 85–86
Concealment and avoidance, 58–
    65
Confidence, 28
Conformity, 66–67
Connecticut, University of, 24
Consciousness-raising, 40
Cook, Constance Eberhart, 181
Counseling, lack of, 87
Counselors, 78
  roles of, 87
Cox, Harvey, 47
Crisis, 29

Critical choice points, 35–52, 42–
    45
  bypassed, 169
  recognition of, 49

D

Dating, by accomplished women,
    128
Denmark, Florence, 31
Divorce, 132
  increase in, and women's move-
    ment, 127
Dole, Elizabeth, 123
Dunn, Mary Maples, 162

E

Eating disorders, 89
Eating problems, 89
Elder, George, 30
Elitism, 84–85
Emotional breakdown, 65
Employment
  male preference, 67
  menial, 37
  opportunities, 114
  post-World-War-II pressure to
    leave, 37
  reentering job market, 152–
    167
Entrepreneurship, 125
Environment versus genetics, 27
Erikson, Erik, 29
Excellence factor, slowing effect
    on, 171
Expectations
  living up to own, 40
  and personal desires, 46–47

societal and family, 45–47
of society, 90

F

Failure, explanations of, 41
"Father figures," 68
Fathers
  absent, 68
  approving, 69–71
  daughters and, 68–69
  three types of, 68
Fear of depriving children of personal imprint, 150
Female role models, 96
Feminine Mystique, The, 39
Finances, responsibility for, 130
Finn, Chester, 26
Fordham University, 157
Freedom to choose, 47–48
Friedan, Betty, 39, 167
Friendships, 82–83
  for emotional support, 94–95
  useful for business, 94
Frozen in place, 44
  warning signs of, 48

G

Gardner, Howard, 26
G. C. Jung Institute, 101
Gershwin, George, 144
Gifted women, failure to meet potential, 32
Gilligan, Carol, 60
Glass ceiling, 119
Goals, 174
Good girl syndrome, 53–58, 66
Goodman, Ellen, 17

Grandmothers, 71–72
Great Depression, 36, 79, 145, 154
Guidubaldi, John, 150

H

Hagen, Rosie, 18
Hagen, Uta, 36, 63
Handy, Charles, 163
Happiness, more recent graduates and, 40–41
Hayes, Helen, 36
Headhunters, 122
Healy, Bernadine, 181
Heilbrun, Carolyn G., 74
Hellman, Lillian, 63
Hillman, James, 101
Hoffman, Lois W., 150
Homosexuality, 137
Horn, John, 26
Hunter College, 15
  entrance requirements, 75–76
  as refuge, 76–81
Hunter College High School, 13, 24
  Alumnae Association, 31
Hunter College Junior High School, 14
Hunter study, 31
Hunter, Thomas, 75

I

Independence, of women, 130–33
Inner self, ways to recapture, 74
"Innovative Developmental Theory Specific to Women, An,"
  two main goals of, 31

Insecurities, hiding, 89
Intelligence
    denial of superiority, 32–
        34
    indications of, 27
    superiority defined, 25
Intelligence quotient (IQ),
    25
Interviews, 35
In Transition, 170
Isolation at top, 118–20

K

Kutner, Lawrence, 138

L

Labor, division of, 133–35
Lack of commitment syndrome,
    129
Lansing, Sherry, 125
Leadership
    preparation for, 94–96
    and risk-taking, 49
    training for women, 146
Levant, Oscar, 144
Levinson, Daniel, 29
Life-cycle theory, 30
Life stages, 29, 42–45
    of adult woman, 43
    and major external event, 30
    movement within, 43
London Business School, 163
Loneliness and isolation, 42
Love
    and marriage, 126–39
    women in, 127–30
Low, Iolanda E., 181

M

McCarthy, Karen, 31
Males
    employment preference, 67
    portion in world, 42
Male stereotypes, 124–25
Male students, 84
Management, bias toward women
    in, 115
Management positions, playing
    politics, 117–18
Marriage
    old-style, 133
    and power, 134
    social pressure for, 138
Mehr, Marilyn, 13, 16, 17, 19–
    20, 24
Mentors, 120–22
Milholland, Inez, 144
Millay, Edna St. Vincent,
    144
Misbehavior, 66
Missing excellence factor, 24
    possible reason for, 47
    roots of, 71–72
Money, 130
Monogamy, 130
Mothers
    as competition and role model,
        59–60
    and daughters' vocations, 108
    work of, 146

N

Networking, 122–23
New York University, 63
Nondecisions, series of, 46,
    109

O

Options, 88
Oxford, 157
Ozick, Cynthia, 181

P

Past, recapturing, 156–61
Pay, equality in, 103, 116, 124
Perfectionism, 66
Potential, unfulfilled, 41–42
Power
  definition of, 134
  women and, 119
P.S. 3, 14
Psychological development, of
  women, 29
Psychotherapy, 65

Q

Questionnaire, 31

R

Radicalism of late 1960s, 99
Recognition, 65
Rees, Minna Spiegel, 181
Reis, Sally M., 24
Relationships, and power, 134
Religion, 157
Resentment, single biggest source
  of, 133
Resumers, 161–65
Richman, Julia, 144
Riesman, David, 163
Risk-avoidance, 104
  in adolescence, 173

Risk-taking, 66, 88
Role models, 47
  lack of, 95
  professional, 120

S

Scholarships, 63
Self-image, of Hunter College
  women, 35–36
Sexuality, 43, 129
Shalala, Donna, 31
Shanker, Al, 15
Sheehy, Gail, 29
Shneidman, Edwin, 165
Singlehood, choosing, 135–39
Sleeping princess syndrome, 103–
  107
"Smartness"
  indications of, 25–28
  label, 85
Smith College, 162
Social change, increased hope and
  opportunity, 41
Social expectations, as a problem,
  40
Social life, marriage and, 136
Social obligations, 95
Social system, challenge to, 47
Spearman, Charles, 25
Sports and athletics, 96
Stanford Binet Test, 26
Stanford University, 23
State University of New York at
  Stony Brook, 161
Stern, William, 25
Straight arrow, 101–3
"Street-smarts", 28
Strengths and talents, lack of as-
  sessment of, 34

Subjects of interviews, 50–52
Substance abuse, 89–90
Successful women, traits of, 73

T

Teachers, 78
  alliance with, 58
Teenage girls, denial of abilities,
  60–61
Terman, Lewis, 23, 25, 73, 165,
  170
  reason for missing excellence,
  24
  study by, 23–24
Two-parent families, 99

U

United Federation of Teachers, 15
United Nations Speakers Research
  Committee, 146
University of California at Los
  Angeles, 165
University of Southern California,
  15, 26
  Faculty Research and Innova-
  tion Fund, 13
U.S. Office of Education, 26

V

Vaillant, Caroline O., 166
Vaillant, George E., 29, 166

W

WAND (Women Against Nuclear
  Destruction), 17
Wasserstein, Wendy, 179
Waters, Professor, 16
Women's movement, and divorce,
  127
Work
  choosing, 97–113
  as incidental to marriage and
  children, 97
  types of, 38
Working mothers
  example of, 150
  as the norm, 151
World War II, as monumental
  event, 37

Z

Zeitgeist, effect on goals and
  choices, 36–39
Zeller, Belle, 181